EPIC

AN AROUND-THE-WORLD JOURNEY
THROUGH CHRISTIAN HISTORY

TIM CHALLIES

ZONDERVAN
REFLECTIVE

ZONDERVAN REFLECTIVE

Epic: An Around-the-World Journey through Christian History
Copyright © 2020 by Tim Challies

ISBN 978-0-310-32904-6 (softcover)

ISBN 978-0-310-59171-9 (ebook)

Requests for information should be addressed to:
Zondervan, *3900 Sparks Dr. SE, Grand Rapids, Michigan 49546*

Unless otherwise noted, all images were taken by and belong to the author.

Published in association with the literary agency of Wolgemuth & Associates, Inc.

Cover design: Ordinary Folk & Eleena Bakrie
Interior design: Kait Lamphere

Printed in the United States of America

19 20 21 22 23 24 25 26 27 28 29 /LSC/ 20 19 18 17 16 15 14 13 12 11 10 9 8 7 6 5 4 3 2 1

CONTENTS

Statistics

Countries:	24
Continents:	6
Flights:	75
Miles:	180,000
Museums:	80

INTRODUCTION

It began with a breakfast.

I had received an email message from a stranger who mentioned he was passing through town and would like to meet me for breakfast. He said he would like to speak with me about money matters, which struck me as a little suspicious and made me more than a little uncomfortable. But hey, free breakfast. I accepted his invitation.

Over bacon and eggs, he shared with me that he represented a group of Christian businessmen who had enjoyed some of my writing and work. They wanted to know if they could help support something new that I was interested in doing.

"If you could take on any project, and money was no object, what would you want to do?"

I knew exactly what I'd do. Just the evening before, I had completed a proposal that had taken me several months to put together, a project so ambitious that I was sure it could never be more than a dream. For the past few years, I had felt a deep longing to explore the roots of my Christian faith. I had wanted to experience the places where significant events in the history of Christianity had occurred, to see and hear and touch the objects that continued to serve as reminders of these pivotal moments and key characters. I had questions to ask. Where did Christianity come from? How did a small movement made up of Jewish men and women grow so fast and spread throughout the entire known world? Who were the people behind this movement? What were the crucial moments that defined it? And how do I, as a twenty-first-century follower of Christ, fit into this epic story?

I love to read history, and I had devoured more books than I could count, looking for answers to my questions. But for this project I wanted to do more than read. I wanted to go. I wanted to explore. I wanted to experience it myself. To see where these people had lived. To experience what it was like to stand where they had stood. Since many of these events happened long ago and the people involved were long dead, I knew that I would need to focus on the objects that remained—those key artifacts that had been preserved. I wanted to "listen" to the objects to hear what I could learn from them, trusting that if I listened well, each one would tell me a different story. My hope was that by listening to the small stories told by these remnants of Christian history, I would begin to understand the larger story and its epic unfolding.[1]

I wanted to "experience" the history of Christianity.

The first step had been choosing the events and characters that were of significance and interest. After endless hours of research, I had drawn up a list of key cities and countries where I could find the objects that would tell me this story. Some choices were simple. I knew I'd need to visit Jerusalem, the city where it all began. I'd travel to Rome, the hub of the Christian church for centuries. As a Protestant Christian,

Stephen McCaskell, who traveled the world with me

I'd have to spend time in Germany where the Reformation began, and travel to England where the great modern missionary movement was founded. And if I wanted a truly global history of Christianity, I'd need to head east to India and China where today countless millions of people confess the name of Jesus Christ. I'd need to go south to Africa and South America where the Christian faith has put down deep roots over the past two centuries. I researched different churches and libraries I could visit, looking for museums that might contain some of the precious artifacts I wanted to see. I mapped out an itinerary spanning twenty-five countries and covering every continent.[2] Everything was ready, but it was all just a dream. I knew I could never afford such a journey.

But now, here I was the very next day, sitting at breakfast across the table from someone who had just asked me to tell him my dream. I didn't hesitate.

"I'd travel the world to search for historical objects that tell the story of Christianity."

And with that, my journey began. A few days later, the money was in the bank and I was frantically arranging interviews with experts and scholars, scheduling tours of museums great and small, and booking long-haul flights to distant lands. Over the course of a very memorable year, I journeyed north and south, east and west. I traveled to Israel to see where Christianity began, to England to find the earliest fragment of the New Testament, to Scotland to trace the roots of a great missionary movement,

A note about my methodology. My focus for this journey was on historical objects, not buildings or locations. I also wanted to avoid statues, markers, and memorials that had been constructed after the fact. I wanted to focus on original, historical artifacts. I also wanted to focus on objects that are available to the public, not locked away in archives and available only to scholars or researchers.

You will undoubtedly notice that some great historical figures and movements are absent. Obviously I had to be selective to keep this book a manageable size, so that's one reason for the absences. Other times, though, it's because none of their objects remain or because they are inaccessible.

Finally, the original vision was to create only a book, but in the early stages I met filmmaker Stephen McCaskell, who caught the vision for the project and decided to travel with me to film a documentary. That has been published alongside the book and is complementary to it. The book focuses on what I found, and the documentary focuses on how I found it.

to Zambia to learn how the gospel spread to the heart of Africa, to India to learn about the lasting work of a remarkable woman, and to my own hometown to find unexpected links to the past. I spent time with Christians in almost every country I visited, and I attended worship services on every continent. And just as I had hoped, I found exactly the kind of objects I had wanted to see. I discovered links to the past, historical artifacts I could see and study and sometimes even touch and hold, each telling me a different chapter of a much greater story.

In this book and the video series that accompanies it, I hope to bring you with me on that journey of searching and finding. Together we will listen to these voices of the past tell us the epic story of what God has done and continues to do in our world today.

Welcome to the history of Christianity, told in a way you've never seen or heard before.

1

AUGUSTUS OF PRIMA PORTA

I'm thankful a friend had warned me I should buy my tickets for the Vatican Museums well in advance. Although I arrived early in the day, the sun was already scorching and the line extended more than two blocks. Hundreds of people waited in the heat, accosted on every side by Rome's ubiquitous hustlers and vendors. Ticket in hand, I was ushered to the front of the line.

The Vatican houses one of the world's great museums—a host of priceless art and artifacts—and it rewards those who proceed at a plodding pace. But I had arrived on a mission and would leave the meandering for another time. My mind was set on the object I had flown more than four thousand miles to see.

The Braccio Nuovo is a long gallery lined on both sides with ancient busts and sculptures, and the highlight of the collection is a magnificent statue called *Augustus of Prima Porta*. At least, that's what I had been told. Today, inexplicably, the gate to the Braccio Nuovo was shut and locked. I couldn't get in. I pleaded my case with the security guard, but he turned his back on me and walked away. I stood for a few moments gazing through the locked gates, trying to catch a glimpse of *Augustus*, but he was hidden in an alcove. Dejected, I wandered off to explore the rest of the museum. Being unable to view the first object on my journey seemed a poor start for my grand project.

A few hours later, I came to the end of a long loop through the museums and spotted an employee arranging a display. He looked to be friendlier than the security guard, so I decided to try once more. He spoke little English and I spoke not a word of Italian, but I somehow managed to communicate what I had come to see. "Follow," he said, and moments later I was ushered past the protesting security guard into the gallery to see *Augustus*. For a few minutes, I was able to stand, look, and listen to what he had to say to me.

Born Gaius Octavius, Augustus was the great-nephew and heir of the famous Roman emperor Julius Caesar. Following his uncle's assassination, Augustus successfully defeated those opposed to Caesar and overcame all challenges to his power. In 27 BC the Senate acclaimed Augustus *Imperator Caesar Divi Filius Augustus*—"Emperor Caesar Exalted One Son of God." He would rule for more than forty years and would be the most acclaimed ruler in Rome's long and storied history. The great poet Virgil would write of him, "Behold the man! Behold the promised one! You know him—Augustus Caesar, the son of a god. He is predestined to power."[1]

Through political skill and clever maneuvering, Augustus ushered in a time of peace and stability that historians now refer to as the Pax Romana, or "Roman Peace." This was a golden age for Roman culture, science, and architecture. What Augustus created during his rule was so powerful and effective that this peace would endure for over two hundred years. It would enable the Roman Empire to overcome a succession of strong opponents from outside the empire as well as weak rulers from within.

But the Pax Romana did not bring peace for *all* people. Although Rome had rest from civil war and serious internal challenges to power, its rulers continued to assert and expand their military might over the known world. Under Julius Caesar Rome had become the dominant power in western Europe, and under the rule of Augustus its armies continued their march, expanding through eastern Europe, northern Africa, and the Middle East.[2]

The Pax Romana, with its questionable "peace," was significant to me because I knew it provided the context for the dawning of the Christian faith. I remembered that Luke, Christianity's earliest historian, began his account of the birth of Jesus of Nazareth by recording, "In those days Caesar Augustus issued a decree that a census should be taken of the entire Roman world" (Luke 2:1). The birthplace of the Christ, Bethlehem of Galilee, was a small town in a province subject to Rome and its emperor.

A view of St. Peter's from
Castel Sant'Angelo

The statue of *Augustus of Prima Porta* in the Vatican Museums showed me the emperor at the very height of his power. Like any good politician, Augustus protected his image carefully, using it to convey something of his power. So while the statue may not be an entirely accurate portrayal of the man as he would have appeared in person, it gave me a picture of the man as he wished to be seen, revered, and remembered.[3] He appears young, athletic, powerful. His face is youthful and handsome, his right arm is raised as if he is giving an oration, and his left leg is bent as if he is striding forward. Here is a man with total power, total confidence in his accomplishments and abilities. His breastplate is covered with symbolic imagery, including a depiction of a barbarian ruler handing a military standard to a Roman general. Twenty-six years before Augustus's reign, Rome had suffered a shocking and shameful defeat at the hands of the Parthians, and this image depicts the great diplomatic triumph through which Augustus restored Rome's honor. Although every ruler before him had failed to vanquish the Parthian menace through military conquest, Augustus was able to neutralize the threat through diplomatic maneuvers. Here I saw the Parthians returning the Roman battle standard they had taken a generation before. Rome's great triumph and great peace are clearly the work of its great emperor.[4]

Under Augustus's rule Rome not only extended its empire but also consolidated and strengthened it. As Roman armies conquered

Augustus of Prima Porta
Till Niermann/Wikimedia Commons, PD-US

new people, officials followed the armies and constructed an infrastructure that could support a mighty empire. The pirates who had once terrorized the seas were nearly eradicated, any bandits or rebels that had made travel unsafe were hunted down and destroyed, and new trading ports and cities sprang up around the Mediterranean. Carefully constructed roads connected one province to the next, and soon it was said, "All roads lead to Rome." These great projects were meant to serve Rome's military

WHILE IN ROME

As you continue to read this book, you will learn about a few more interesting objects in Rome. But let me tell you about one more within the Vatican Museums. If you visit the Raphael Rooms, take a careful look at the giant painting *Disputation over the Most Holy Sacrament*. If you look in just the right spot, immediately below the book lying on the lower step, you'll see the name "Luther" roughly carved into it. This is a strange leftover from the time of the Reformation when German soldiers sacked Rome and left behind this little memento of their visit—this token of their break with Rome.

and its economy, but they inadvertently served a far greater purpose. The ports that were intended to accommodate traders and soldiers also served the earliest missionaries. The roads that allowed Rome to conquer with sword and spear also allowed Christian men and women to conquer the world in a very different way and with a very different weapon. During his rule, Augustus even advocated a form of religious tolerance, allowing other faiths to coexist with the established Roman polytheism. His Pax Romana provided the infrastructure and a measure of stability that would allow the Christian faith to spread far and fast.

Yet in *Augustus of Prima Porta* I could also see the roots of what would become the early church's most deadly challenge. At *Augustus*'s right side is Cupid sitting upon a dolphin, a reminder to his subjects that he, like Julius Caesar before him, was descended from Venus, the goddess of love. His bare feet both symbolize and declare his divinity, for where a mere man goes to war wearing boots, a god strides into battle barefoot. Augustus was not only a mighty emperor but a son of the gods.[5]

Augustus died when Jesus was still a boy, perhaps around the time Jesus visited the temple and chose to remain behind without his parents (see Luke 2:41–52). The *Augustus of Prima Porta* statue was created to declare and affirm all his claims to divinity and, by extension, the claims of the emperors that would follow him. As Christians took advantage of the Pax Romana to spread their own gospel message, a message declaring there was but one God and one way to God, they would inevitably come into conflict with the "gospel" of these divine emperors. Either Jesus was *the* Son of God, or the emperors were sons of gods. Both could not stand together.

Upon his death Augustus was succeeded by Tiberius, who in turn was succeeded by later emperors whose reigns would be short and in many cases forgettable. What remained consistent for the next two centuries was the dominance of Rome and the power of its emperor. The Pax Romana would survive for many generations, and with it the conditions that would continue to aid the spread of the gospel of Jesus Christ. But where Augustus had allowed other faiths, many of his successors would suppress them. Jesus's earliest followers soon faced imprisonment and even death. They walked the roads of Rome and passed through its ports, but often at a high cost.

Although the *Augustus of Prima Porta* statue is now nearly two thousand years old, in seeing it I could catch a brief glimpse of a different world, the world in which the great story of Jesus and the early church was born. In Jesus's parting words to his most trusted followers, he commanded that they should go into all the world with the message of his gospel (Matthew 28:16–20). Yet he also warned them that the gospel's advance would be met with fierce persecution (Matthew 10:16–33). In

Augustus of Prima Porta I saw the providence of God in bringing about the right conditions for the Christian faith to spread quickly and widely, fulfilling the words of Jesus. And I also saw the seeds of the adversity that would accompany and purify that faith. As Tertullian would say a century later, persecuted by one of Augustus's successors, this adversity to the gospel, often requiring the blood of martyrs, is like a seed that causes the church to grow.

As my time listening and reflecting came to a close, I was ushered out of the Braccio Nuovo, grateful to have seen *Augustus* and to have pondered his unexpected role in the history of a faith founded twenty years after his death.

I had hoped to see another key object in the Vatican Museums that day, but before I tell you about it, we need to travel to another destination—thirteen hundred miles to the northwest. There we'll turn our attention to a tiny scrap of parchment that, in its own way, is now one of the most precious documents in the world.

2

JOHN RYLANDS
MANUSCRIPT P52

In 1920 Dr. B. P. Grenfell was traveling through Egypt when he came across a collection of ancient papyri. He purchased them on behalf of the John Rylands Library in Manchester, England, and the fragments were dutifully numbered and added to the library's collection, but they were quickly set aside and nearly forgotten. Fourteen years would pass until another man, Colin H. Roberts, a fellow of St. John's College in Oxford, would spend time with the papyri collection and happen upon a tiny fragment that had been assigned the number 52. P52 was quite small—all of fifty-three square centimeters in size. It had only a few faded Greek characters written on its front and back. But as Roberts translated those characters and analyzed their style, he saw something amazing. This tiny fragment had tremendous historical significance. It quickly became the subject of intense historical research and scholarly debate, until eventually scholars arrived at a consensus: P52 was a treasure worthy of permanent display, the crown jewel of the John Rylands Library.[1]

I arrived at the library on a cool spring morning just as it opened its doors for the day. I was surprised to learn that the library not only houses an array of books and manuscripts but also a diverse and curious collection of artifacts. And it houses this curious collection quite curiously, at least to my eye. The little piece of parchment rediscovered years ago by Colin Roberts is located in a room filled with books and objects spanning a variety of topics and of different ages, all with seemingly little connection to one another. Immediately beside the parchment is a display featuring obstetrical tools, of all things. Yet the fragment itself is carefully encased, protected in a climate-controlled cabinet where it remains on near-permanent display. Having come so far to see this tiny object, I was eager to learn more about it, to study it, and to carefully consider its significance. But as I did so, I noticed that few of the people browsing the collection that morning gave it more than a quick glance. It's easy to understand why. The P52 papyri fragment is but a tiny scrap of shredded, discarded papyrus, just 8.9 by 6 centimeters at its widest points. Why would anyone give it a second glance, much less travel halfway around the world to view it? Was I wasting my time?

No. The P52 fragment is significant, not only because of what it is, but because of what it represents. P52 is an ancient piece of the Bible. As I listened, it told me about God's great work in giving us his Word and in preserving it through the millennia.

The Christian faith is entirely and unapologetically dependent on God's revelation of himself in the Bible. Christians believe that over many years and through many different people, God used human authors to record his divine words, a phenomenon commonly referred to as "inspiration." In the New Testament, some of these authors wrote a biography of Jesus. Some wrote personal letters directed to a specific audience. One wrote a history of the early church. It was only natural that after these Scriptures had been written, they were widely shared. The young pastor Timothy, the recipient of two letters from his mentor Paul, shared Paul's fatherly wisdom with other young pastors. The church in Ephesus, also the recipient of a letter from Paul, shared that letter with other nearby congregations. Those who wanted to know about the life of Jesus were drawn to the account written by his friend John or the account penned by the historian Luke. As the Christian faith grew and spread, there was increasing demand for these Scriptures, which meant they needed to be copied and recopied and widely distributed. This process, in turn, brought about a proliferation of manuscripts.

Yet with the proliferation of manuscripts came a complicating factor. These were years before printing presses, photocopiers, or digital media, and every word of each manuscript had to be copied by hand, one character at a time. When the books were copied out in this way, differences inevitably began to appear.

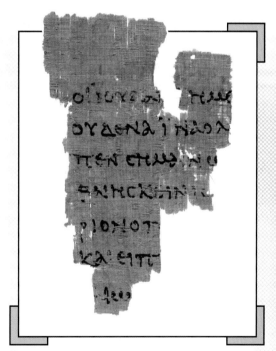

P52 fragment

Reproduced by courtesy of the University librarian and director, The John Rylands University Library, The University of Manchester

The majority of such changes were minor and unintentional—a skipped letter, a missed word, a repeated line. Some changes were intentional but meant to be helpful—a scribe might substitute an obscure word with a common one, or he might add words or phrases to clarify the text. And after the four gospels became widely known, scribes might spot differences between them and attempt to bring harmony by changing the wording of on=e to match another.

In the church's earliest days, these copies could be verified against the original manuscripts, but over time those originals disappeared until only the handwritten copies remained. Eventually even those first copies of the copies were lost to the process of time, through use and decay. All that remains today are copies of copies of copies, and few of these perfectly match one another. All of this raises a conundrum: if we are entirely and unapologetically dependent on the Bible but we don't have original copies, how can we have any real confidence in the words we read and believe? How can we be confident that the Bible we possess today is truly the one God inspired? This is where we benefit from the scholarly discipline of textual criticism.

Textual critics are highly skilled experts and scholars who examine and evaluate the surviving manuscripts to accurately reproduce the original text. And in understanding this, we begin to see the importance of this little fragment of papyrus encased in glass in John Rylands Library.

When Colin H. Roberts studied the manuscript, he immediately recognized it as a tiny fragment of the book of John. It contains words from the account of Jesus's trial before Pilate—John 18:31–33 on the front and John 18:37–38 on the back. The Greek characters in bold are those that have survived and can be read. They are followed by the English translation.[2]

Front:

ΟΙ ΙΟΥΔΑΙΟΙ ΗΜΕΙΝ ΟΥΚ ΕΞΕΣΤΙΝ ΑΠΟΚΤΕΙΝΑΙ **the Jews, "For us** it is not permitted to kill
ΟΥΔΕΝΑ ΙΝΑ Ο ΛΟΓΟΣ ΤΟΥ ΙΗΣΟΥ ΠΛΗΡΩΘΗ **anyone," so that the w**ord of Jesus might be
   ΟΝ ΕΙ-   fulfilled, which he
ΠΕΝ ΣΗΜΑΙΝΩΝ ΠΟΙΩ ΘΑΝΑΤΩ ΗΜΕΛΛΕΝ ΑΠΟ- sp**oke signifyin**g what kind of death he was going to
ΘΝΗΣΚΕΙΝ ΙΣΗΛΘΕΝ ΟΥΝ ΠΑΛΙΝ ΕΙΣ ΤΟ ΠΡΑΙΤΩ- **die. En**tered therefore again into the Praeto-
ΡΙΟΝ Ο ΠΙΛΑΤΟΣ ΚΑΙ ΕΦΩΝΗΣΕΝ ΤΟΝ ΙΗΣΟΥΝ **rium P**ilate and summoned Jesus
ΚΑΙ ΕΙΠΕΝ ΑΥΤΩ ΣΥ ΕΙ Ο ΒΑΣΙΛΕΥΣ ΤΩΝ ΙΟΥ- **and sa**id to him, "Thou art king of the
ΔΑΙΩΝ **Jews?"**

Back:

ΒΑΣΙΛΕΥΣ ΕΙΜΙ ΕΓΩ ΕΙΣ ΤΟ**ΥΤΟ ΓΕΓΕΝΝΗΜΑΙ**
ΚΑΙ (ΕΙΣ ΤΟΥΤΟ) ΕΛΗΛΥΘΑ ΕΙΣ ΤΟΝ ΚΟ**ΣΜΟΝ**
 ΙΝΑ ΜΑΡΤΥ-
ΡΗΣΩ ΤΗ ΑΛΗΘΕΙΑ ΠΑΣ Ο ΩΝ **ΕΚ ΤΗΣ ΑΛΗΘΕΙ**-
ΑΣ ΑΚΟΥΕΙ ΜΟΥ ΤΗΣ ΦΩΝΗΣ **ΛΕΓΕΙ ΑΥΤΩ**
Ο ΠΙΛΑΤΟΣ ΤΙ ΕΣΤΙΝ ΑΛΗΘΕΙΑ Κ**ΑΙ ΤΟΥΤΟ**
ΕΙΠΩΝ ΠΑΛΙΝ ΕΞΗΛΘΕΝ ΠΡΟΣ **ΤΟΥΣ** ΙΟΥ-
ΔΑΙΟΥΣ ΚΑΙ ΛΕΓΕΙ ΑΥΤΟΙΣ ΕΓΩ ΟΥ**ΔΕΜΙ**ΑΝ
ΕΥΡΙΣΚΩ ΕΝ ΑΥΤΩ ΑΙΤΙΑΝ[3]

a King I am. For **this I have been born**
and (for this) I have come into the **world so that I**
 would testify
to the truth. Everyone who is **of the truth**
hears of me my voice." **Said to him**
Pilate, "What is truth?" **and this**
having said, again he went out unto **the Jews**
and said to them, "I find **not one**
fault in him."

Based on the style of the script used, Roberts dated the fragment to the first half of the second century, and though there has been much debate since that claim was first made, the broad consensus of scholars is that he was correct. Most scholars place the manuscript somewhere between AD 125 and 150, making it the oldest surviving copy of any portion of the New Testament.[4] Think about that. This little scrap of papyrus is our oldest historical link to the New Testament Scriptures. And in its own way, it represents the thousands of manuscripts and fragments of manuscripts that led to the Bible we have today. As we will see in later chapters, my journey would eventually lead me past hundreds of Bibles and pieces of Bibles, but this tiny fragment of papyrus would be, by far, the oldest I would encounter.

The P52 manuscript fragment is significant not only because of its content but also because of where it was found. Bruce Metzger once described its importance in this way: "Just as Robinson Crusoe, seeing but a single footprint in the sand, concluded that another human being, with two feet, was present on the island with him, so P52 proves the existence and use of the Fourth Gospel during the first half of the second century in a provincial town along the Nile, far removed from its traditional place of composition (Ephesus in Asia Minor)."[5] From this fragment we can deduce that already in the first half of the second century Christians were living along the Nile, and they were reading the very same words John had written the century before, the same words that we read today in different translations. Just as we value those words and pore over them to promote understanding and application, so did our brothers and sisters, the earliest Christian believers. Picture a Christian in ancient Egypt reading the account of Jesus's trial and crucifixion, marveling at God's grace, and praying with faith that Christ would soon return. P52 may not be the most substantial of the ancient manuscripts, and certainly it is not the one most critical to assembling the original text of the Bible. Yet it is a significant link to the past—to my past and yours. It is an object I could look at and listen to and grow in my convictions about the providence of God in preserving his words.

If faith comes through hearing and hearing through the Word of God (Romans 10:17), we are reminded that you and I are Christians today only because God has preserved his Word, the Bible. And he has preserved his Word through copy after copy of the original manuscripts, even through small fragments of papyrus like this one. For such a little scrap of discarded papyrus, it has an amazing story to tell.

And on that note, we head back to Rome, the source and destination of many of the letters that form our Bibles today.

A QUICK LOOK:
THE PILATE STONE

I said we would head back to Rome, and we will do so shortly, but first I'd like to make a brief stop in Jerusalem. In the preceding chapter, I said that the Christian faith is entirely and unapologetically dependent on God's revelation of himself in the Bible. And this is true. But our faith is not a blind or ridiculous faith; it's not a hopeful but naive shot in the dark. Rather, it is a faith that is corroborated by evidence. When Paul wrote about the importance of Jesus's resurrection as a fundamental fact of the Christian faith, he reminded his readers that Jesus "appeared to more than five hundred of the brothers and sisters at the same time, most of whom are still living, though some have fallen asleep" (1 Corinthians 15:6). He appealed to his readers to have confidence in the resurrection not only on the basis of his authority as an apostle ("Because I said so") but also on the basis of verifiable evidence ("Go and do your own research"). It's as if he told them, "Don't believe me? Five hundred people saw the resurrected Jesus. Go talk to them, and they'll assure you!"

In much the same way, we have confidence in the Bible today not only because of how it testifies to itself and not only because of how the Holy Spirit convicts us of its truthfulness, though both of these are crucial. We also have confidence in the Bible because what it lays out as facts can be corroborated through historical evidence. In fact, as the historical record continues to become clear through archaeology, our confidence in the historicity of the Bible only ever continues to grow.

Any study of Christian history will show that time and again skeptics have insisted that elements of the Bible cannot be true because

Snapping photos of the Pilate Stone
© *Stephen McCaskell*

21

the historical record is silent. This was exactly the case with the Roman governor Pontius Pilate, who plays a particularly important and tragic role in the death of Jesus. For many years skeptics insisted that he was a fabrication of the early Christians, and they backed their claim by showing that no one had found archaeological evidence of his existence. "If he really existed, why haven't we found any original references to him?" This all changed in 1961 when an Italian archaeologist was excavating ancient Caesarea and found a limestone block that formed part of a staircase. This block had been recycled from an earlier building that had been torn down, for on the back of it was an inscription, a dedication. Although some characters were missing, it was not difficult to reconstruct the wording:

[in honor of] Tiberius
[Pon]tius Pilate
[Praef]ect of Judea[1]

The stone had once dedicated the building, probably a temple, to Tiberius Caesar. This was the first, and to that point the only, object that bore his name, but it was enough. Now no one could legitimately doubt that Pilate had indeed existed and that he had indeed governed Judea. The Bible had once again been vindicated.

I visited the Israel Museum and focused on the wonderful *Cradle of Christianity* exhibit, which contains a number of fascinating items. It displays a crucifixion nail, still attached to a piece of bone, similar to the nails that pinned Jesus to

The Pilot Stone, the Israel Museum, Jerusalem
© 2018 by Zondervan

his cross. It displays a placard from the temple, warning gentiles not to approach the place where only Jews could go. But, best of all, it proudly displays the Pilate Stone. And as I stood before the stone and studied its words, grateful for my high school teacher Dr. Helder and those many Latin classes, it confirmed to me anew that the Bible is true and reliable, that I can trust it to guide my life and doctrine. It assured me that every part of the Bible is true, including its descriptions of historical events and characters. If I could prove the Bible wrong in one part—such as the nonexistence of an important character—I would have reason to doubt the whole thing. I would have legitimate reason to consider it all unreliable, nonfactual, and fallible. But as the archaeological evidence compounds, so, too, does my trust in God's infallible, inerrant, reliable Word.

3

ALEXAMENOS GRAFFITO

Rome is famous as the city built on seven hills. The Palatine Hill sits at the center of it all, rising above what remains of the Roman Forum on the one side and the Circus Maximus on the other. It has been the setting for many historic moments—which is why it merits its own museum, the Palatine Antiquarium Museum. Some of the exhibits display models of early villages that predate the founding of Rome. Others hold relics of ancient temples and other buildings that once adorned the hill. Among these relics, secured on a wall, is an ancient piece of graffiti.

But—would you believe it?—the museum housing the graffiti was closed and locked on the day I visited. I'd put countless hours into planning a trip to Italy—plotting out flights, hotels, and local transportation, and securing guides, and one of the objects I had come to see was unavailable during my visit. They say that those who fail to plan plan to fail, but this experience made it clear that even the best planning isn't enough. My visit to the Vatican Museums had left me unexpectedly scrambling, searching for a way to see *Augustus of Prima Porta*. And now, as I arrived at the Palatine Antiquarium Museum, I discovered that it, too, was closed. Again, no explanation was given. An Italian friend shrugged and said, "That's Italy for you." My planning had been solid; I'd researched times and days. I had done everything I could. But for some reason I was experiencing a string of seemingly random closures.[1]

Eventually I had to count my losses, retreat, and organize a second trip to Rome. So now, several months later, I was here again, standing before the Palatine Antiquarium Museum. This time, thankfully, the doors were unlocked and open. I had come a long way and gone to a lot of bother just to see a piece of graffiti. But it was worth it.

Alexamenos graffiti, Palatine Antiquarium, Rome (litho)

© Zev Radovan/Bridgeman Images

This particular piece of graffiti had been carved into plaster and was discovered in 1857 during archaeological excavations at the site. It was soon dubbed the Alexamenos graffito.[2] It appears old and rather faded, and the original design is difficult to discern, yet a close look or a careful tracing of the carved section of wall reveals two figures and a string of Greek characters. To the left is a man raising his hand in adoration, a posture of worship or prayer. To his side, rising above him, is a second man suspended from a cross. Crucifixions were very common in Rome, and this second man looks as you might expect—arms outstretched, pinned to a crossbar. His feet are planted on a platform, and he is wearing some kind of garment that is covering his lower body. But what distinguishes this man from other crucified criminals is that while he has the body of a man, he has the head of a donkey. The inscription near the drawing sarcastically explains the scene, "Alexamenos sebetai theon," "Alexamenos worships his God." Here is Jesus, the crucified Savior, and Alexamenos, one of his committed followers.

Historians date this graffiti to approximately AD 200, which makes it the earliest surviving depiction of Jesus hanging on a cross. This fact alone gives it great significance. Yet it is also important to note that this is not a religious icon meant to elicit awe or worship. The graffiti is a mockery of an ancient Christian and the God he worshiped. It is a mockery of any so-called God who would die the shameful death of a criminal and any person who would be naive and foolish enough to worship him.

The first object I visited was *Augustus of Prima Porta*, who reminded me that Christianity was birthed in a time when Rome was the world's dominant power. In considering that statue of Caesar Augustus, Rome's first and greatest emperor, I saw the context for Christianity's rapid expansion. Yet at the same time, I saw the seed of her early persecution. The relationship between Rome and the Christian faith was always complicated and often shifting. There were times of peace and freedom when Christians were allowed to express their allegiance to Jesus. There were also times when Christians faced systemic persecution, when they were hunted down and put to death for daring to reject the gods of Rome and the divinity of the Roman emperor.

Yet even in times free from government persecution, Christians were still mocked and belittled for their beliefs and practices. Even in the best times, they stood out for denying the gods others worshiped and for worshiping a God others denied—or mocked. They were considered foolish and unsophisticated for worshiping a God who had been put to death as a common criminal. Strange to our modern way of thinking, they were labeled *atheists* for their steadfast refusal to acknowledge many gods and for their stubborn insistence that there was just one, true God.

While we don't know much about Alexamenos, we know that he was a Christian, a man who proclaimed that Jesus is Lord. He worshiped a God who became a man, who lived out his life within the confines of the Roman Empire, and who endured the most painful and shameful death devised by the cruelest minds of that time. And along with countless other Christians before and after him, Alexamenos was mocked for what he believed. Living approximately 150 years before Alexamenos, the apostle Paul had written that "the message of the cross is foolishness to those who are perishing, but to us who are being saved it is the power of God" (1 Corinthians 1:18). Every Christian knows the shame of believing in this truth about God. It's something so unusual, so unexpected, so unfathomable, and seemingly foolish. Yet every person who claims to follow Christ believes that this act

To gain entry to the Palatine Antiquarian Museum, you'll need to purchase a pass for the Palatine Hill. After visiting the museum, be sure to walk down the hill to visit the Roman Forum and other ancient buildings. Don't miss the Arch of Titus, which is an amazing historical monument that depicts the Roman siege and sack of Jerusalem in AD 70. Look especially for the reliefs of the various temple implements being carried away by the conquerors.

of folly is in reality the very power of God, a sacrificial act that accomplishes our salvation.

Many Christians in the world today can attest that the call to follow Jesus is a call to bear shame and to face mockery, to be the butt of jokes and an object of scorn. This is a very different kind of suffering from those who faced the lions or the stake in Rome's nearby Colosseum, but it is still a form of suffering. And in this ancient graffiti, we remember that what is true today—even if it comes in different forms—has been true of those who have followed Christ throughout history. Our ancient brother Alexamenos knew the shame and foolishness of worshiping a crucified God; he was mocked for raising his hand—and pledging his life—to a Savior on a cross.

This ancient graffiti had something to say to me that day. It told me that the history of the church has always involved bearing shame and facing persecution for the sake of the Crucified One. It told me that every Christian enters into a fellowship of suffering with Christ himself and with each of his followers. Feeling fellowship with this ancient brother, this ancient fellow follower of Jesus Christ, was challenging and strangely comforting. May I be willing to raise my hands in worship, as he did, even in the face of mockery or outright persecution.

Having seen this graffiti and having explored the Arch of Titus, I made my way back to the Vatican Museums to find another ancient, important object that shows how Christian doctrine developed in those early years.

Ancient ruins at the Roman Forum

4
DOGMATIC SARCOPHAGUS

The Vatican Museums in Rome house a vast collection of ancient objects, many of them related to the early history of the Christian church. Among the various museums is the Pius-Christian Museum, and I traveled there to experience our next object. Remarkably intact despite its age, I soon located an intricately carved sarcophagus—a box designed to hold human remains.[1] This particular box was discovered in Rome's basilica di San Paolo fuori le Mura during its restoration in the 1800s. Historians date it to somewhere between AD 330 and 350.[2]

The outside of the sarcophagus is divided into upper and lower tiers, and each tier is carved all around with biblical imagery drawn from both the Old and New Testaments. Among the scenes recreated along the upper tier are God giving his creation mandate to Adam, the wedding at Cana, and the miracle of the loaves and fish. Along the lower tier, you can find the arrival of the magi to worship the baby Jesus, the healing of the blind man, Jesus foretelling Peter's denial, and Peter baptizing his jailers. In the middle of it all is an image of the Christian couple who originally commissioned this sarcophagus to be their final resting place.[3]

Although it is interesting enough to look at, the sarcophagus itself is rather unremarkable, as several similar ones are displayed all around it within the Pius-Christian Museum. No great historical figure was buried in it. But there is something that sets this one apart, something that helped me to better understand the history of Christianity. It's the scene carved at the top left of the upper tier—the creation of Eve.

Looking closely at the carved scene, I could see Adam lying on the ground in what appears to be a deep sleep. Eve stands beside him with the hand of God on her head as God brings her

Dogmatic Sarcophagus, Vatican Museums, Rome
Sailko/Wikimedia Commons, CC BY 3.0

to life. And there above her, easy to miss except with a close study, is God.[4] He is pictured as three identical figures in a representation of the shared act of creation by Father, Son, and Holy Spirit. And this is why this particular image is so significant. This scene on the sarcophagus, now known as the Dogmatic Sarcophagus or Trinity Sarcophagus, is a visual representation of early Trinitarian theology. This portrayal of the three members of the Godhead working together in creation has a unique historical significance. And the three being portrayed identically holds additional significance.

Early in the fourth century, Emperor Constantine was triumphant in battle, ending a time of civil war in the Roman Empire and uniting all of the empire under his rule. Constantine was also the first of Rome's emperors to claim Christianity as his faith, and with his ascension to rule, he ended state persecution of Christian believers.[5] However, even as the grave external threat of Roman persecution was removed, the Christian church soon faced an even greater threat from within its own ranks. The threat came in the form of Arius, a gifted and persuasive presbyter who oversaw Baucalis, a parish of Alexandria (in modern-day Egypt). Arius claimed that the Father was God, but the Son was not. Tim Dowley has helpfully condensed Arius's teaching on the nature of God to one short paragraph.

Arius claimed that the Father alone was really God; the Son was essentially different from his Father. The Son did not possess by nature or right any of the divine qualities of immortality, sovereignty, perfect wisdom, goodness and purity. He did not exist before he was begotten by the Father, who produced him as a creature. Yet as the creator of the rest of creation, the Son existed "apart from time before all things." Nevertheless, he did not share in the being of God the Father and did not know him perfectly.[6]

Arius taught that Jesus was not the eternal God. He was not coequal with the Father but rather the first and greatest of the Father's *created* beings. Many Christians immediately understood the implications of denying the divinity of Jesus Christ. Denying this core belief undermined his standing as the redeemer of humanity, for to be the perfect mediator between God and man, Jesus had to be both fully human and fully divine.[7] Although a church council at Alexandria examined Arius and excommunicated him, he continued to teach and gain influence. Soon a substantial number of Christians had been swayed by the teachings of Arius, and a major rift threatened to undermine the fledgling church. Constantine saw that his empire was split over what he considered a minor matter of doctrine, and he demanded that church leaders convene a council to examine the various teachings and solve the problem.

The Council of Nicaea, now seen as the first of the great Christian councils, was convened in AD 325. There Arius was quickly determined to fall outside the bounds of church teaching.

He was labeled unorthodox, denounced as a heretic, and exiled to Illyricum (a Roman province made up of parts of modern-day Serbia and Croatia). The council's greater task was to create a precise statement of Trinitarian theology. While the Bible was clear in teaching that God is triune, the precise relationship between the persons of the Trinity had never been formally and officially defined by a church council, a gathering of all Christian leaders. The council's task was to carefully and faithfully clarify the doctrine and show how it was understood from the teaching of Scripture. They distilled all of their discussion into just 170 words, what we now call the Nicene Creed:

> We believe in one God, the Father, Almighty, maker of all things visible and invisible; And in one Lord Jesus Christ, the Son of God, begotten of the Father, only-begotten, that is, from the substance (*ousia*) of the Father; God from God, Light from Light, Very God from Very God, begotten not made, of one substance (*homoousios*, consubstantial) with the Father, through whom all things were made, both in heaven and on earth; who for us men and for our salvation came down and was incarnate, was made man, suffered, and rose again on the third day, ascended into heaven, and is coming to judge the living and the dead; And in the Holy Spirit.
>
> And those who say: "There was a time when he was not," and: "Before he was begotten he was not," and: "He came into being from

nothing," or those who pretend that the Son of God is "Of another substance (*hypostasis*), or essence (*ousia*)" [than the Father] or "created" or "alterable" or "mutable," the catholic and apostolic church places under a curse.[8]

As I stood before the Dogmatic Sarcophagus in a Roman museum, I knew that I was looking at a distinctly Nicene representation of the Trinity. The Father, Son, and Holy Spirit are all portrayed, an indication that while there is but one God, this God is three persons. Father, Son, and Holy Spirit are portrayed identically, an indication that they are "one substance,"

A little church beneath the towering Dolomite Mountains, Italy

equal in divinity and working in harmony. Had Arianism triumphed at Nicaea, this box would have been carved very differently, and the history of the church might have proceeded along a very different path. Perhaps we would have seen the Father portrayed slightly larger than the Son, looming over him. Perhaps the Spirit would be absent altogether. Perhaps this scene would be the creation of the Son, not the creation of Eve. But because the church took time to carefully define its beliefs according to the standard of the Bible, I could see Father, Son, and Holy Spirit portrayed as equals on this small box.

The Arian controversy was just one of many debates in the early church necessitating both councils (to discuss and debate the matter) and creeds (to summarize and teach the doctrinal conclusions). These creeds and councils helped define the beliefs of the Christian church by clarifying the teachings of the apostles against challenges to those teachings. These clarifications were used to determine who was in and who was out, who was considered orthodox and who was heretical. They protected the church and its doctrine through their precise statements of biblical theology and their strict warnings to those who would deviate from orthodoxy. Although the Nicene Creed was not the final word on Trinitarian theology, it remains a remarkably accurate declaration of what the Bible teaches about the Godhead. Christians around the world have been reciting its words for more than sixteen centuries.

The Dogmatic Sarcophagus has survived the centuries as a visual representation of the teachings of those councils and creeds. If I was tempted to take for granted the long, hard, and prayerful labor of searching the Scriptures to determine what the Bible teaches about the relationship of Father, Son, and Holy Spirit, this box reminded me that today's Christians owe a large debt of gratitude to our Christian forebears. It called me to be grateful for the way the Lord worked through the men who labored at those ancient councils. We stand on their work and continue to build on their legacy.

And now I needed to head east to both Scotland and Ireland to track down one of the visual and literary treasures of the Christian faith, one that would combine the best art of its time with the best Book of all time.

5

BOOK OF KELLS

The next object in our journey through history took me to the western coastline of Scotland—one of my favorite countries in the whole world. After landing in Edinburgh and teaching myself to drive on the "wrong" side of the road, I made my way across the Isle of Mull, where I boarded a tiny ferry to go the short distance from Fionnphort to a place called Baile Mór on the island of Iona. I was here to learn more about one of the world's most precious books, the Book of Kells.

Although the book itself is now displayed in Dublin, Ireland, I wanted to learn as much as I could about its origins, to see where this famous book had originally been written. I passed through the sleepy village and strolled to the ancient Iona Abbey, once a ruin of fallen walls but now carefully rebuilt. In the early 800s, this abbey was a bustling center of Christian mission, dispatching preachers across Scotland and Northern England. While those missionaries were out preaching the gospel message to those who had never heard it, others worked in the monastery's scriptorium, carefully copying the Scriptures. Standing before the abbey, I paused and tried to imagine the hustle and bustle of that once thriving mission.[1]

Sadly, tragedy struck. Vikings raided and pillaged the island, and many of the abbey's monks were killed. Under the threat of ongoing violence, the surviving monks fled to Ireland's County Meath and settled into a new abbey. They took with them their precious books, and among the volumes they carried to Ireland is the one we now call the Book of Kells.[2] After spending some time exploring the abbey and learning more about the book's origins, I was ready to see the book itself.

At this point you may be wondering, *Why travel all the way from Ontario, Canada, to western Scotland, and then to Dublin to see a book?* Well, as I mentioned, the Book of Kells is

Slemish Mountain, where St. Patrick worked as a shepherd for a number of years

a unique book. There is nothing quite like it anywhere in the world. It's a manuscript containing the four gospels in Latin, and it dates all the way back to around AD 800. What first stands out to those who view it is its sheer beauty. The pages are made of fine vellum, and nearly every page is adorned with beautiful, intricately designed illustrations. The Book of Kells is an ancient Bible, but it is also a stunning work of art.

What's equally amazing is that the book has survived through the ages. After its move to Kells, it survived another century of attacks on the abbey from the nearby Danes. After Danish raids, the book was stolen and, before it could be retrieved, suffered significant water damage.

At one point the gold and jewel-encrusted cover was torn off and lost, along with a few of its opening pages. In modern times the book was poorly rebound and the pages harshly cropped. Clearly, it has not always been treated as the treasure it is. Yet it has survived largely intact, and despite the damage to the book over time, it remains stunning in its beauty.[3] In 1661 the book arrived at its present home in Trinity College in Dublin, where more than five hundred thousand visitors come to see it each year. I was grateful and glad to be among them, to have an opportunity to step out of the near-constant wind and rain of the Irish spring to spend time with a treasured artifact of Christian history.

The Arrest of Christ, Gospel of St. Matthew, from the Book of Kells, MS 58 *folio* 114r (vellum), ninth century

The Board of Trinity College, Dublin, Ireland/Bridgeman Images

The Book of Kells has been bound into four volumes, one for each of the gospels. On any given day, two of them are placed on display. One of the volumes is typically opened to a major illustration, while the other shows two pages of text. Both volumes are kept behind thick glass and under constant guard. Although the room is almost always busy, visitors are welcome to stand and gaze at the books as long as they wish. The library has also carefully and skillfully scanned the entire work, and they have created both an app and a website so that those who wish to see more of the manuscript can study it in high definition from anywhere in the world.[4]

The manuscript is well worth a close look. Only a handful of its 680 pages lack ornamentation, and most pages have multiple illuminations of letters. Several pages are almost entirely covered in decoration and illustration. These illuminations feature multiple colors, which at the time necessitated using rare and expensive imported dyes. The artistry is so fine that some details can only be appreciated under close magnification.[5] Of all the illuminated manuscripts produced in medieval Europe that have survived to our time, this is certainly the finest. It is well worth a visit.

The Book of Kells is significant because it stands as a beautifully preserved example of history's most important and enduring Bible translation. No, I'm not referring to the King James Version of the Bible, though it, too, has a place in Christian history and in this book. In the fourth century, Pope Damasus I had commissioned a man named Jerome to revise and update the Old Latin translation of the gospels. But Jerome went far beyond his original mandate and ended up revising the entire Bible.[6] His work would later be called the Vulgate, which is Latin for "common version." The Vulgate would endure as the standard and accepted translation of Scripture until around the time of the Reformation, when several of the Reformers would begin to create new translations in different languages from the foundational Greek and Hebrew texts. But the Vulgate stands apart, for from its writing in the fourth century to the sixteenth-century Reformation, to quote the Bible was to quote the Vulgate.[7]

The Book of Kells is equally significant as a demonstration of the spread and preservation of the Christian faith. As we saw earlier, the Roman Empire had at one time been the seat and center of Christianity, beginning in Rome and then shifting to Constantinople. But as the centuries passed, the Roman church became increasingly corrupt, bound to tradition rather than Scripture, and increasingly obsessed with earthly riches and power. God chose to preserve his Word and his people in other lands, especially after the stunning collapse of the Roman Empire in the fifth century. By this time Christianity had spread to Britain, where missionaries like Saint Patrick would carry the gospel from Britain to Ireland.

Eventually men like Saint Columba, in whose honor the Book of Kells was created, carried it from Ireland to Scotland. Over time and through this faithful labor, the gospel began to spread from land to land, reaching people of different tribes and tongues.

As I studied the Book of Kells under thick glass, it told me that though the ancient church began as a local movement among the Jewish people, God intended the message of Jesus to go global. In the Book of Kells, I was reminded that though there were times when the Christian faith did not thrive, the Lord still preserved his people, his witness, and his Book. Through these ages, God's people patiently waited for a new day, a spark that would ignite the faith with new force. To begin that part of the story, I needed to travel to the mainland of Europe and journey to southern Germany.

6

JAN HUS'S CELL DOOR

The Protestant Reformation shook the church in the sixteenth century, but it did not erupt in a void. It was but one among many reforming movements that spanned the preceding centuries. Just as the incoming tide creeps a bit higher with each breaking wave, each of these movements advanced the truth a little further until reaching a breaking point in the sixteenth century. Four hundred years before Martin Luther nailed his Ninety-Five Theses to the door of a church in Germany, Peter Waldo ignited a powerful movement of lay preachers throughout southern France and northern Italy. Years before John Calvin wrote his *Institutes*, a man named John Wycliffe was translating the Bible into English and another man, Jan Hus, was preaching against the errors of the Catholic Church in Bohemia. Each of these men prepared the way for a tidal wave of change we now refer to as the Reformation. Each lived in great peril and endured great persecution.

As I read and studied each of these figures, it was Jan Hus who most captured my imagination, so I set out to find what remained of his life and to learn what I could of his death. Hus was born around 1370 in the small town of Husinec, Bohemia—located in the modern-day Czech Republic. He received a good education and by his midtwenties had advanced degrees and a teaching position at the University of Prague. In 1402 he was asked to be the preacher at Bethlehem Chapel, close to the university. He accepted the position and, as he began to preach week by week, encountered the writings of John Wycliffe. But how did Wycliffe's writings travel from England to faraway Bohemia?[1]

In 1382 Richard II of England married Anne of Bohemia. Their marriage was a political move aimed at uniting England and Bohemia, two nations that considered France a common enemy. This newfound unity opened the way for travel and communication to pass between the two nations, including for a number of scholars. As Bohemians studied in England, they encountered the philosophical and theological teachings of Wycliffe and brought them back to Prague.[2] Eventually Jan Hus encountered these teachings, and they changed his life.

Hus became a devotee of Wycliffe. He began to read the Bible with fresh eyes, and he adopted much of Wycliffe's theology, including the belief that the church is made up of all of God's elect for all of time and that the church's rightful head is Christ rather than the pope. Because the chapel where Hus preached was in such close proximity to Bohemia's foremost university, he gained tremendous influence over a generation of young scholars.[3] Soon the city rang with cries for the church to reform its theology and practice.

By 1409 the pope had decided enough was enough. He commanded the archbishop of Prague to crack down on the growing unrest, and the authorities prohibited Hus from preaching at Bethlehem Chapel. He refused to comply with their orders and was soon excommunicated by church authorities. Then, in 1412, Prague was threatened with an interdict from the pope that would prohibit the celebration of the Mass across the whole city. Hus realized it was time for him to leave, so he took his preaching to rural areas. Yet his influence continued to grow.

In 1414 Sigismund of Hungary, the Holy Roman emperor, convened the Council of Constance (modern-day Konstanz, Germany).

Hus museum in Constance (Konstanz), Germany
CTK/Alamy Stock Photo

Although the primary purpose of the council was to resolve the embarrassing Papal Schism, a forty-year period in which two or sometimes even three men claimed the papacy, it was also meant to address the cries for reform coming from men like Wycliffe and Hus. Hus was summoned to the council under Sigismund's promise of safe conduct. However, Catholic authorities had him arrested, insisting they were under no obligation to honor promises that had been made to a dangerous heretic. Hus was held in a prison within the local Dominican monastery under brutal conditions.[4]

That monastery itself no longer stands, but an interesting piece of the old building has been preserved. And though a number of exhibits and memorials in Hus's honor can be seen in his native Czech Republic, the Hus Museum in Konstanz, Germany, houses many of the most intriguing objects related to his life and death. Set in a small building in a quaint and busy shopping district, it uses placards and exhibits to tell the story of Hus's life and influence. I flipped through the guest book and saw that the museum had welcomed visitors from around the globe, many of them hailing from the Czech Republic. A narrow staircase led me to the second floor, where one object stood out: the door of the cell that once confined him. Near the door are the stone and chain that fastened him within that cell. After the death of Jan Hus, his followers saw fit to save these items to honor his memory. Seeing them was both stirring and chilling as I considered what it might have been

like for Hus to suffer, confined for nearly eight long months in such terrible conditions.

The cell door is composed of thick hardwood, now stained and darkened with age. Great iron bands brace it, adding the appearance of tremendous strength. The sliding lock that once held the door fast is still in place, and beneath it stands a stone with an iron loop used to hold a chain to restrain the prisoner and keep him from escaping. The scene is austere, a reminder of the deplorable conditions in which Hus was held captive for those long, cold, and uncomfortable months. His mistreatment was enough to break his health, but it could not break his spirit. By the time he appeared before the council, he was sick and weak but still resolute. Inevitably, he was condemned to die, and the bishops committed his soul to the devil. As they did so, Hus had a simply reply: "And I commit myself to my most gracious Lord Jesus."[5]

On July 6, 1415, Jan Hus was unfastened from the rock that confined him and was led through that door for the final time. He went to his death physically broken but with a spirit of confidence and a joyful solemnity. Although he was offered a last-minute pardon if he would recant his heresies, he remained steadfast to the end, declaring, "In the truth of the gospel I have written, taught, and preached; today I will gladly die."[6] He was tied to a stake and burned to death. His ashes were thrown into the Rhine River to ensure there could be no lasting place of honor in his name. His death sparked a civil war that raged on for fourteen years until it was finally settled in a peace agreement that allowed the Bohemian church to remain within Catholicism while granting them special privileges. The Bohemian church remained distinct in the years following and, with the outbreak of the Reformation, quickly folded itself into the growing Protestant movement.[7] When Luther protested the selling of indulgences a hundred years later, he remarked that he was merely building on the work that Jan Hus had begun.

Seeing these objects—a door, chains, and a rock—reminded me that the road to reformation was long and difficult, paved with suffering. They reminded me that Hus and others like him were willing to pay a price, to give up their lives for their beliefs. And they reminded me that the gospel we celebrate and cherish today has been preserved and retrieved with blood from a power-corrupted institution. I left the museum sobered but anxious to trace the continuation of the work that Hus had a part in beginning. To do that, I would not need to go far.

7

GUTENBERG BIBLE

Johannes Gutenberg is one of those rare individuals who quite literally changed the world. When A&E's *Biography* closed out the second millennium with their list of the one hundred most influential people of the past thousand years, Gutenberg's name was at the very top of the list, ahead of names like Isaac Newton, Charles Darwin, Christopher Columbus, Karl Marx, and others whose names and legacies might be far more familiar to the masses. This German inventor changed the world in the fifteenth century through his invention of the movable-type printing press.

Gutenberg was born around the year 1400. I say "around" that time because history has recorded few facts about his early life. We know he was first a goldsmith and then an inventor who fell on hard times. It was not until he was near the age of forty that Gutenberg began to experiment with printing. He may have come up with the idea for the printing press while living in Strasbourg, but by 1450 we know that he was settled in the city of Mainz, Germany, and operating a rudimentary press. The first items he produced were probably simple poems and grammars, but he soon conceived the idea of printing an entire Bible. The first Gutenberg Bibles came off his presses in 1455.[1]

The most remarkable part of Gutenberg's invention was not the press itself but the type. Until that point in history, almost all books were handwritten, painstakingly copied by scribes so that a single Bible might take years to complete. Block printing was also becoming popular, but it, too, was slow since it required an entire page to be carved into a wooden block before being coated in ink and pressed onto paper. Because of the onerous production process, books were quite rare and very expensive. Gutenberg understood that printing could be made exponentially faster by splitting the text into its most basic parts and using movable blocks of letters and punctuation marks. Sets of these characters could then be arranged to form a page of words, which could then produce any number of facsimiles.[2]

Gutenberg designed a screw-type press that he adapted from wine-making equipment. He modified it so he could quickly slide paper in and out and easily squeeze water from the paper after the printing was complete. None of Gutenberg's presses survive today, but a handful of copies of his first works remain in existence. The first complete book to come from his press was his Bible—the one we know today as the Gutenberg Bible.

Considering the value and scarcity of Gutenberg Bibles, finding one is surprisingly easy. Historians believe Gutenberg printed somewhere between 150 and 180 copies. Today forty-nine are known to have survived, twenty-one of them complete. Holding a Gutenberg Bible is a mark of distinction for any great museum or library, so copies can be found in many global cities, such as London and Paris, New York and Berlin, Vienna and Moscow. But perhaps the best place to see one is at the Gutenberg Museum in Mainz, Germany, Gutenberg's hometown.[3] I visited Mainz near the close of a cold winter's day and lingered to see the rest of the museum's collection of some of the earliest works ever to emerge from a movable-type printing press. These included a number of printed indulgences,

Stephen and me walking from one filming location to another

© James Kuan

The Gutenberg Bible ca. 1453 printed by Johannes Gutenberg in Mainz, Germany

Peter Horree/Alamy Stock Photo

the likes of which would soon ignite a young monk named Martin Luther to protest against the abuses of the Roman Catholic Church. The museum curators have carefully reproduced Gutenberg's early press to demonstrate how he created his books, and I enjoyed seeing the demonstration of how the press worked. But that was just icing on the cake. The real reason for my visit was Gutenberg's greatest printed work, the Bible.

The Gutenberg Bible is an edition of the Latin Vulgate, similar to the Book of Kells. As mentioned earlier, this was the standard translation for much of the time leading up to the Reformation. It is printed in two volumes and is over twelve hundred pages. It has little adornment when compared to the illuminated Bibles of the medieval era, but it is still remarkable for its artistry and especially for the lavish characters that begin individual books and chapters. The volumes in the Gutenberg Museum are housed in a dark, climate-controlled room, laid under thick glass, and kept under strict surveillance. Don't try sneaking in a camera! Cameras are not allowed and *will* be spotted. But do spend some time looking at the pages and considering what they represent. This is one of the rarest, most treasured books in the world.

Although the volumes on display are in some ways unremarkable, especially when compared with the Book of Kells, what filled my thoughts as I looked at them was the significance of the technology that produced them. Movable type, combined with the press, provided a quantum leap forward in printing and publishing. Although for a time this new technology remained a trade secret, in 1462 Mainz was plundered and the secrets of Gutenberg became common knowledge. Within twenty years printing presses were set up all over Europe. Tim Dowley writes, "It was the most momentous invention since the stirrup, and a revolutionary step forward in technology. Like the invention of gunpowder (rediscovered at about the same time), the application of print to book-production held a tremendous potential for good and evil in subsequent history."[4]

As the cost of book production plummeted, the availability of books skyrocketed. What was written in print now had the power to spread much faster and much farther than anything before it (which is analogous to how the world has been transformed more recently through the rise of social media and the instantaneous communication it allows). Gutenberg's press was crucial in giving birth to the Renaissance, the Scientific Revolution, and the Protestant Reformation. The availability of printed material and the desire to read it also led to a great increase in literacy. The world was forever transformed.

Looking back at history from our vantage point, we can see how God used this invention for his purposes, just as he had the rise of Caesar Augustus and the Pax Romana, and just as he would later use other great innovations like the radio and the internet. As I stood in that dark room and "listened" to the Gutenberg Bible, I heard it tell me that God was preparing the world for a great spiritual upheaval, a great Reformation. The Gutenberg Bible is significant not so much because of its physical form, but because of the technology that produced it. Men and women were beginning to proclaim the gospel and translate the Bible into the common languages. And now a technology had been invented that had the power to spread the knowledge of God faster and wider than ever before. The ingredients for an explosive moment were slowly but steadily coming together.

Before I could turn my attention to that great Reformation, I had to make a quick drive across the border to Switzerland to consider one additional significant artifact.

8

ERASMUS'S NEW TESTAMENT

One of the most important Reformation-era figures would become a hero to Protestants and a villain to many Catholics, even though he lived and died a son of the Roman Catholic Church. In some ways he was too Protestant for the pope and too Catholic for a Reformer like Martin Luther. He taught and influenced generations of scholars, pastors, and theologians. Many of them remained faithful to Catholicism, while others abandoned the Catholic Church for the growing Protestant movement. Although he lived through the first two decades of the Reformation, his most important contributions were made before it even began. I'm referring to the great scholar Desiderius Erasmus Roterodamus.

No telling of church history can be complete without accounting for Erasmus's life and influence, and especially his impact in recovering the Greek Scriptures. A copy of his great work

Novum Testamentum omne is the focal point of the Reformation exhibit in Zurich's Swiss National Museum. Desiderius Erasmus was born in Rotterdam, Holland, in 1466, the illegitimate son of a Roman Catholic priest. He was given a fine education at monastic schools and, upon completing his education, was ordained as a priest. Three years later he began studies at the University of Paris, where he was exposed to Renaissance humanism.[1] Seeds were planted in Paris that would later make him a fierce opponent of excess and superstition within the Catholic Church. He soon traveled to England and was persuaded by John Colet, an English scholar, to study the New Testament. Erasmus believed that to properly understand the New Testament, he would first need to learn Greek, and so he began an intense, three-year study of the language.[2] By the end of his studies, he was not

Switzerland has more than its fair share of beautiful church buildings!

© Aileen Challies

only fluent in Greek but had become an eminent scholar of the language.

I need to pause briefly to distinguish what is referred to as Renaissance humanism from our contemporary use of the term. Modern-day humanism is a system of thought that replaces divine revelation with human reason and highlights human potential. It is committed to finding a rational or scientific explanation for every phenomenon.[3] But our contemporary use of this term bears almost no resemblance to the earlier use of the term, for Renaissance humanism was a movement away from medieval scholasticism in favor of ancient Greek and Roman thought. If that doesn't mean much to you, think of it as a return to classical literature and philosophy,

a return to the cultural influences communicated through the languages of Latin and Greek.[4] Erasmus became a Greek scholar so that he would have access to these ancient texts, and one of the texts that became particularly interesting to him was the New Testament.

At this time, the late fifteenth century, the Latin Vulgate was still the sole authorized Bible of the Roman Catholic Church, even though it had been translated over a thousand years earlier and Latin had long since become a dead language to all but scholars and clerics. In the course of his studies of the original Greek texts, Erasmus came to see that the Latin translation had a number of inaccuracies. He believed the language could be polished and updated, so he set out to create a

Beginning of Romans from *Novum Testamentum omne*, 1519

Princeton Theological Seminary Library

typographical errors, but the second and subsequent editions were much superior.[5] Although Erasmus's intention was to create a new Latin translation, it is the Greek that would prove far more important and enduring.

A decade after Erasmus died, the Council of Trent condemned his New Testament and reaffirmed that the older Vulgate of Jerome was to remain the official text of the Roman Catholic Church. But by then it was too late. Erasmus's work had already been widely disseminated, and the recovered Greek text allowed Bibles to be translated directly from the original text into other languages, rather than having to be translated from the Vulgate. As one biographer of Erasmus has said, "[His Greek text] was the fountain and source from which flowed the new translations into the vernaculars which like rivers irrigated the dry lands of the mediaeval Church and made them blossom into a more enlightened and lovely form of religion."[6]

Although first editions of Erasmus's work still exist in a number of collections, I was most interested to track down the second, corrected edition, which had been retitled the *Novum Testamentum omne*. There is one of these volumes in the collection of the Swiss National Museum in Zurich, a two-column New Testament with the Greek in the left column and Erasmus's fresh Latin translation in the right. It's a relatively small volume, about the size of today's common hardcover, but it stands in a dedicated case that's impossible to miss in the center of a room in the museum dedicated

new Latin text. To do this, he first had to collect all the available Greek manuscripts he could find. Despite the relative scarcity of manuscripts at his disposal, he ended up with a remarkably good selection to draw from.

In 1516 the first printed edition of Erasmus's translation rolled off the Basel-based presses of John Froben under the title *Novum Instrumentum omne*. The book was a two-column work with the Greek source text in one column and Erasmus's fresh Latin translation beside it. This first edition, rushed to print, contained many unfortunate to the Reformation.[7] The opening page of each book is lavishly illustrated, though only in black and white, as are the drop caps that begin the various books. Both times I visited the museum, the book was open to the first chapter of Romans, suggesting that this may be its permanent state. I know just enough Latin and Greek to read the first few lines and could make out the familiar words and cadence of Paul's opening greeting. "Paul, a servant of Christ Jesus, called to be an apostle, set apart for the gospel of God." And while we don't know much about the provenance of this particular volume, we do know it matches the one Luther relied on when he did his own translation of the New Testament into German. In fact, Erasmus's work in its various editions would be the basis for almost every translation from the sixteenth to the nineteenth centuries, including William Tyndale's influential English translation.

At this point I felt like I needed to take a few moments to consolidate what I had learned so far about this period between the early church and the Protestant Reformation. Pre-Reformers like Jan Hus had begun to speak out against the abuses of the Roman Catholic Church, attempting to recover the gospel message and attempting to give the Bible to the people, as best they could. The printing press had provided the ability to disseminate ideas with much greater speed and at far lower cost. And now, in the midst of these shifts, the Greek New Testament text had been recovered and collated, allowing for far more accurate translations into the common tongues of different nations. The framework for the Reformation was in place. All that remained was a spark that would light a great fire. That spark ignited in the nearby country of Germany, so I once again had to cross the border and travel north.

9

INDULGENCE BOX

The city of Wittenberg, Germany, had been freshly painted before I arrived. That year was a celebration of the five-hundredth anniversary of the Protestant Reformation, and Wittenberg was one of several German towns that had done some sprucing up for the occasion. Each city was trying to put on its best in preparation for the deluge of tourists who would use this occasion to make their own pilgrimage to the birthplace of the Reformation. I paid a brief visit to the cathedral where Martin Luther is buried, but found that a concert was about to begin, and I was quickly ushered out. Walking down the street, I came upon the home of the great theologian Philip Melanchthon, where I endured an unfortunate (and historically untenable) presentation about his latent homosexuality. Looking for more helpful and reliable information, I walked around the corner and came to the Lutherhaus museum, the former home of Martin Luther.

Lutherhaus is located within an Augustinian monastery once known as the Black Cloister. Martin Luther spent much of his life here, first as a monk and later as a pastor, a husband, and a father. It was here he had his life-changing "tower experience" and wrote his Ninety-Five Theses. This was where he led the beginnings of a reformation movement and eventually settled into married life, where he delivered his famous table talks and wrote so many of the books and missives that would come to define his legacy. It was here, more than anywhere else, that he dedicated himself to studying the Bible and understanding its gospel message. Today the Lutherhaus is one of the world's premier museums dedicated to the Protestant Reformation.[1] Much of the building, particularly the "Luther Hall," has been preserved or restored in a manner close to its original state.

Spread throughout the museum is a collection of artifacts related to Luther's life and times, and among the collection is a small, nondescript iron chest. This chest (and many others like it) have played an outsized role in the history of the church. These small boxes are visible evidence of the corruption that forced Luther's hand and, in their own way, set into motion a series of events that would change the world. They tell a story if we are willing to hear it!

Martin Luther was born in November 1483 in Eisleben, Saxony, in modern-day Germany. His father was an ambitious and accomplished man who wanted his son to succeed in the world, so he sent young Martin to school, where he studied Latin and was trained in a regimented religious life. In 1501 Luther entered the University of Erfurt and proved to be a brilliant student, earning both a bachelor's and master's degree within just four years. He graduated and enrolled in law school and was on the path to becoming a lawyer when, in the summer of 1505, he was caught outside on the side of a road during a terrible thunderstorm. Terrified by a nearby lightning strike, he cried out to Saint Anne that if he survived the storm, he would become a monk. Luther did survive, and though he regretted his rash vow, he was a man of integrity and held to his promise. He dropped out of law school, sold his books, and against the urgings of his father, entered an Augustinian monastery.[2]

Luther dedicated himself to his calling as a monk. He would later say, "If anyone could have gained heaven as a monk, then I would certainly have done so." He fasted, prayed, studied, went on pilgrimages, and confessed his sins constantly. Yet despite his best efforts, he remained in a state of near-constant despair, unable to find peace or any assurance of God's love and

Castle Church in Wittenberg, Germany, where Martin Luther is buried

acceptance. He continued his academic progress and by October 1512 had earned two more bachelor's degrees and a doctorate of theology. These academic pursuits drove him to study the Bible more in depth, and as he did so he began to see conflicts between what the Scriptures taught and several doctrinal teachings of the Roman Catholic Church, particularly on the doctrine of justification. His studies eventually led him to a shocking discovery: "In Romans, Paul writes of the 'righteousness of God.' This was surprising to him because Luther had

Indulgence box

always understood the reference to 'righteousness' to mean that God was a righteous judge who demanded human righteousness. Instead, Luther began to see that the righteousness spoken of in this letter was not a righteousness given by human beings, but a righteousness from God, given as a gift of God's grace. Luther had discovered (or rather recovered) the doctrine of justification by grace alone—and this discovery set his heart and mind afire."[3]

While Luther was awakening to this new understanding of justification and beginning to grapple with its consequences, the Roman Catholic Church had dispatched Johann Tetzel, a Dominican friar, to Germany. Tetzel was tasked with selling papers called indulgences to raise funds that were needed to rebuild St. Peter's Basilica in Rome.[4] Indulgences were written

promises issued by the church that provided a means for sinners to reduce the punishment God owed them for their sin. Financial contributions were made to the church, which would then draw upon the treasury of merit—the accumulated righteous deeds of Christ and the saints—and credit merit to those individuals, assuring them that the punishment due to their sins had been covered. Although the official word was that indulgences were only meant for those who showed true sorrow and repentance, in reality they were bought and sold as something of a talisman, an insurance policy that would negate the consequences of any sin that had been committed, either knowingly or inadvertently.

Indulgences came to typify the widening gulf between the Roman Catholic Church's teaching on justification and Luther's new, emerging understanding of forgiveness as a free, unmerited gift of grace. Where Luther now held that justification came by faith alone—not as the result of human effort, as something to be earned—the church taught that justification came through a combination of faith and works. Tetzel's indulgences were seen by Luther as a means of purchasing God's grace, and the bartering of something precious, given freely in love, infuriated Luther. Tetzel, with his sales pitches, went so far as to claim that his indulgences could be purchased on behalf of people who were already suffering in purgatory. Who wouldn't be willing to make a contribution that would reduce the purgatorial suffering of their loved ones? A popular rhyme often attributed to him says it best: "When a penny in the coffer rings, a soul from Purgatory springs."

One of these "coffers" used to collect coins for indulgences is now on display in the Lutherhaus museum. Set on the floor near an early printed copy of Luther's Ninety-Five Theses, it is a plain and unadorned metal box, notable only for the coin slot in the lid. But even though it is simple and unremarkable in appearance, it represents a watershed moment in church history. The coins that slid through the slot and into the coffer represented a gospel of salvation by works, a gospel foreign to the Bible, a false gospel. They represented Rome's insistence that the Church had the right and authority to set the terms of repentance, salvation, and the remittance of sin, that the

Church could modify the promise of God and change the key to the kingdom of God, replacing it with a key that would unlock a treasury of merit. Luther had rediscovered the biblical and apostolic doctrine of justification by grace alone through faith alone, and as this teaching spread throughout the church, it became clear that it was in direct conflict with the sale of indulgences and the idea of salvation through meritorious good works.

Luther responded to Tetzel and his indulgences by writing a series of Ninety-Five Theses

The famous doors of the Castle Church in Wittenberg, Germany
© Stephen McCaskell

that outlined his concerns and the nature of true repentance and assurance. Luther nailed these papers to the university chapel's door on October 31, 1517, hoping they would generate discussion and a movement of reform within the church.[5] He certainly had no idea what he had just unleashed. With the aid of the newly invented printing press, his theses were quickly distributed across Germany and Europe, and what had begun as a simple discussion of indulgences soon widened into a scandal that threatened to cause a great rift in Christianity. The Roman Catholic Church would need to respond, and Luther would have to choose whether to recant or stand firm. During the Diet of Worms in 1521, he chose to stand, uttering these bold words, "Unless I am convinced by proofs from Scriptures or by plain and clear reasons and arguments, I can and will not retract. . . . Here I stand. I can do no other. God help me. Amen."[6] The Reformation had begun, and it would soon spread across Germany, then across Europe and to the rest of the world. One of the first countries it would impact, and one of the countries it would impact most deeply, was England, so I needed to return there to pick up the story.

10
TYNDALE NEW TESTAMENT

Not long ago the British ruled an area so vast that it was popularly said that "the sun never sets on the British Empire." As the British explored and colonized, archaeologists followed behind, gathering historical treasures and collecting artifacts and objects. Many of these precious cultural treasures were removed from their original locations, shipped to England, and added to the great museums and libraries of London and other major cities. In this way England came to curate many global treasures related not only to its own history but also to the history of the ancient world. Its museums are second to none.

One of the greatest of these collections, aptly named the Treasures Gallery, is located at the British Library. Here, in this oft-changing collection, I found Codex Sinaiticus, Leonardo da Vinci's notebook, the Magna Carta, Shakespeare's First Folio, and several other amazing works (though I was unable to find Lady Jane Grey's prayer book, a treasure that was not on display just then). The Treasures Gallery is one of the most compact and valuable collections of historical treasures to be found anywhere in the world. And among these great jewels I also found a rare copy of William Tyndale's New Testament, perhaps the most important English book of all time, not only for the development of the nation, but also for its language.

William Tyndale was born in 1494 in Gloucestershire, England, into a wealthy family. Growing up he had the privilege of studying at both Oxford and Cambridge, and proved to be a brilliant scholar, fluent in eight languages. At Cambridge he studied theology, though he later lamented that this study had involved

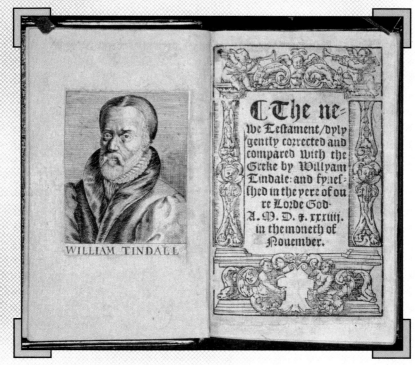

C23.a.5 New Testament, translated from the Greek by William Tyndale, revised
version, published November 1534 in Antwerp, British Library, London

© British Library Board. All Rights Reserved/Bridgeman Images

precious little actual study of the Bible.[1] During his time at Cambridge, he also encountered the teachings of Desiderius Erasmus and became convinced that the Bible alone should serve as the Christian's rule of faith and practice. This meant that every Christian ought to have access to the Bible in his own tongue. Yet as Tyndale began to espouse this viewpoint and align himself with the Reformation that had begun spreading across the continent, he was soon viewed as a dangerous and seditious individual. Undeterred, he persevered in his convictions and continued teaching and studying.[2]

In 1523 Tyndale went to London to seek support from church leaders for a new English translation of the Scriptures, one based on Erasmus's Greek New Testament text. To this point it was rare to find translations of the Bible into English, and the few available were fragmented copies and illegal to possess. Also, they were based on the Vulgate and reflected its inaccuracies and mistranslations. Since no support was forthcoming, and realizing that England would not be a safe place to complete his translation work, Tyndale departed for mainland Europe. He would never again return to his native land.[3] Initially, Tyndale sought Luther's help and settled in Germany, perhaps even in Wittenberg.

By 1525 he had finished his translation of the New Testament and sought to have it printed in Cologne. Sadly, before even a single volume could be printed, the civil and religious authorities learned of it and Tyndale was forced to flee the city, fearing for his life.[4] He traveled to Worms, where the first volumes were printed and quickly smuggled into England, hidden in bales of cloth. Although it was illegal to own or to read a Tyndale Bible, the demand for them was unrelenting.

The volume that can be viewed in the British Library is one of three thousand New Testaments printed and one of only *three* copies to survive to the present day. It is pocket-sized, making it ideal for smuggling and concealing from the authorities. This diminutive size sets it apart from the oversized, authorized Bibles of the day, books that were intended for display on lecterns and pulpits, not for reading by common people. The original binding has been lost and replaced with a new binding in red leather with gold tooling. The interior of the book is beautifully illuminated, with "extra" coloring added by one of its many owners long after the printing.[5]

As with most of the objects I encountered on my journey, the physical book itself is far less important than the words contained on its pages. And it is not simply for printing the Bible that Tyndale is remembered, but for translating the words of Scripture into the common language of his people. As he translated from the original Greek, Tyndale was able to correct many of the weaknesses of the Vulgate. For example, where the Vulgate used the word

The entrance into the British Library
© *Dan Erickson*

"Church," Tyndale used the more accurate term "congregation." Where the Latin spoke of doing "penance," Tyndale called people to "repentance." The Latin "priest" became the English "elder."[6] His translation reflected his Protestant theology, and as the English people read the English Bible for the first time, they were introduced to distinctly Protestant doctrine.

Tyndale's influence was certainly felt in his own day, but also long after his death, through subsequent English translations of the Scriptures. Scholars estimate that between 80 and 85 percent of the King James Version of the New Testament is drawn from Tyndale's translation, along with more than 70 percent of his translation of the Pentateuch.[7] Many words in the Christian lexicon that are commonly known today were coined by Tyndale, including the words *Passover*, *atonement*, *Jehovah*, *scapegoat*, and many more. Many precious and familiar phrases are derived from his translation as well, including "Blessed are they that mourn, for they shall be comforted," "salt of the earth," and "the spirit is willing but the flesh is weak." To say that Tyndale should be credited as one of the foremost inventors and shapers of modern English would not be an overstatement.

After completing his New Testament translation, Tyndale began to translate the Old Testament from Hebrew, and he completed the first five books along with Jonah. After King Henry VIII led the Church of England to split with Rome in 1534, Tyndale moved to Antwerp and began to exercise less caution, but his relaxing of his guard soon led to his imprisonment and death. A friend betrayed him, and he was arrested. After spending more than a year in prison, Tyndale was charged with heresy and treason. On October 6, 1536, he was strangled to death and then burned at the stake. His final words were a prayer: "Lord, open the king of England's eyes." By God's grace his prayer was soon answered, for a mere three years later, King Henry published his "Great Bible." Although the book itself was assembled by Miles Coverdale, the New Testament contained within was based almost entirely on the work of Tyndale.

Early in his life, in the midst of a theological argument with an ignorant clergyman, Tyndale had exclaimed, "I defy the Pope, and all his laws; and if God spares my life, ere many years, I will cause a boy that driveth the plow to know more of the Scriptures than thou dost!"[8] The rest of his life was dedicated to this task, and it was accomplished in his translation of the New Testament. Where the Bible had formerly been available to only the few who had knowledge of Latin, it was now available for even the lowly plowboy to read. That plowboy and countless other English speakers did read it!

At the cost of his life, William Tyndale set God's Word free for the multitudes to read in the English language, and once set free, the Word proved itself living, active, and sharper than any two-edged sword. It left an indelible imprint on the souls of countless individuals, and its impact continues to be felt today. I feel it every time I sit down to read the Bible, to meditate on it, and to feed my soul with its precious truths. This precious copy in the Treasures collection reminds me of the great privilege I enjoy in having the Bible available to me in my mother tongue. While most people in the Treasures Gallery crowd around the works of da Vinci, Lennon and McCartney, and Shakespeare, they are remiss if they do not also pause to consider the much greater significance of this work of Tyndale.

11
CALVIN'S CHAIR

It's possible there is a nation with more natural beauty than the small country of Switzerland, but if there is, I've yet to see it. My journey to listen to the stories told by the significant objects of Christian history eventually led me to visit this nation not once, but twice, and on both of those visits I found myself pausing numerous times to admire the incredible vistas and mountain peaks. From its green, pastoral hills, to the rugged mountains and deep valleys, Switzerland is a stunningly beautiful place. But it's also a nation with a rich Christian history.

Almost every major city in Switzerland houses a church, cathedral, or museum that holds a key to a better understanding of the history of the Christian faith, especially the developing story of the Protestant Reformation. Perhaps chief among those cities is Geneva, which, in its heyday, was regarded by some Protestants as "the perfect school of Christ."

Saint Pierre Cathedral, lying at the center of the city, dates from the twelfth century. Over the years, wars, fires, renovations, and additions have repeatedly transformed the appearance of the church. Today it is the home of a congregation belonging to the Swiss Reformed Church, but it will always be better known as John Calvin's church, for this was the center of his prodigious ministry. Here, within the walls of Saint Pierre, is one of the very few artifacts remaining that can be directly tied to Calvin, one of Protestant Christianity's (and wider Western society's) most important and influential theologians.

In 1517 Martin Luther's posting of the Ninety-Five Theses had sparked the Reformation, and in the years that followed, his "seditious" teachings quickly spread throughout Europe, splitting Western Christianity into two broad streams: Roman Catholicism and Protestantism.

The work Luther had begun was soon picked up by others, but no one would play as crucial a role in defending and systematizing Protestantism as John Calvin. As one historian has said, "If Luther sounded the trumpet for reform, Calvin orchestrated the score by which the Reformation became a part of Western civilization."[1] Calvin's influence not only shaped the Christian church; it profoundly shaped Western civilization for the centuries that followed.

John Calvin's chair
Roy LANGSTAFF/Alamy Stock Photo

Through his writings, his legacy would extend far beyond the nation of Switzerland, reaching France, Scotland, and eventually the ends of the earth.

John Calvin was born in 1509 at Noyon, a town in northern France. From an early age, he had an interest in church matters and intended to become a priest, but his father, believing his son would have better prospects as a lawyer, enrolled him in the University of Orleans to study law. Along the way Calvin became intrigued by humanism and came under the influence of humanist teachers. Yet he also studied and mastered Greek, a skill that would serve him well later in life.[2]

In 1533 the young Calvin first encountered Luther's teachings, and he was suddenly and unexpectedly converted. Later he would remark, "God by a sudden conversion subdued and brought my mind to a teachable frame, which was more hardened in such matters than might have been expected in such a young man."[3] He soon broke ties with the Roman Catholic Church and became a leader within the Parisian Protestant movement. This change of allegiance made him a marked man, and he fled his native France, first traveling to Germany and then to Switzerland. He eventually settled in Basel, intending to lead a quiet life as a scholar, but regular reports of the persecution of Protestants in France aroused his passion—and his pen.

In 1536 Calvin published the first edition of the *Institutes of the Christian Religion*, and it immediately sold well, thrusting him into the limelight and gaining him some unwanted attention. He decided to travel to Strasbourg to go into hiding, but on the journey there he passed through Geneva, where a man named William Farel was waiting for him. Farel was a fellow Frenchman and a preacher who had settled in Switzerland. He made several forceful appeals to Calvin, charging him to remain in Geneva to preach and to provoke reform within the city. Calvin heeded his summons, and except for a short interval during which he was forced out by his church, he remained in the city until his death in 1564.

Calvin was first a preacher who was in the pulpit several times each week, and for as long as he preached in Geneva, he did so at Saint Pierre Cathedral. His preaching was marked by a deep belief in the authority of Scripture, by faith in the presence and power of God in the proclamation of the Word, and by a commitment to sequential, verse-by-verse exposition of God's Word.[4] He modeled a commitment to preaching and a style of preaching that many later preachers would imitate, including his acolyte John Knox.

But today we remember him most as a theologian, as the original "Calvinist." He continued to expand and improve his *Institutes* until it became one of the first and certainly the most enduring Reformation-era theological works. The *Institutes* are still read and treasured today. In fact, it has recently experienced a resurgence of interest and influence.[5]

Castle Chillon, on the shores of Lake Geneva

One of the countless mountain switchbacks in Switzerland

Few relics or objects connected to Calvin's life have survived, at least in part because this was his wish. Calvin was so aware of the power of superstition that he had no desire for his belongings or even his body to be preserved. Today you can walk from Saint Pierre to the nearby Cimetière des Rois (cemetery) and find a tomb with his name engraved on it, but this small monument marks, at best, the general vicinity in which he was buried. No one knows exactly where his body really lies.[6]

Yet one object connected to Calvin's life does still remain, and it can be still seen today: his chair. Calvin's chair sits within the cathedral, settled just underneath the pulpit. It is a simple wooden chair, so unadorned and unremarkable that I had to do a second sweep of the building to find it. Calvin's chair reminded me that the power of his words, whether written or spoken, were derived from his long hours of study. All who heard Calvin and knew him understood that for every hour he stood in the pulpit, he had spent countless more sitting, studying, praying, and seeking to understand and apply God's Word. For every word written in the *Institutes*, Calvin invested many hours in study and contemplation. His preaching ministry, his work as a systematic theologian, and his scholarship all

Here are a few other Reformation sites to visit in history-rich Geneva:

- Cimetière des Rois. Calvin's body is buried here, though no one knows exactly where. As you enter the cemetery, you'll find a map showing where to find his tomb.
- International Museum of the Reformation. It is easily one of the greatest museums dedicated to the Reformation.
- The Reformation Wall. It commemorates some of the key Reformation-era figures in the form of a huge monument.

went hand in hand. He was utterly committed to understanding the Bible so he could obey it and teach others to do the same.

Calvin's sermons and letters, his commentaries and *Institutes*, continue to influence generations of Christians. Calvin lived and died, his pulpit rose and fell, but the gospel he preached and the theology he helped define carry on. His chair aptly speaks of his life and legacy and the necessity of careful and deliberate study of God's Word as the basis for following God's ways and sharing the message with others.

Calvin makes a very different kind of appearance in the next object. While his chair in his cathedral memorializes his importance as a great Reformer, an object in Rome presents him as an arch heretic worthy of the greatest punishments devised by the mind of man or God.

12

THE TRIUMPH OF FAITH OVER HERESY

The Protestant Reformation deeply rocked the Roman Catholic Church. Five hundred years later we know the church survived and remained strong, but at the height of the Reformation, it was not unreasonable to question if the Roman Catholic Church and the papacy could endure the challenges to its teaching and authority. Not surprisingly, the Catholic establishment was not passive in the face of the Reformers' teaching, nor did the church authorities simply accept the growing rift within Christianity. Their response is commonly referred to as the Counter-Reformation, and it was a time of formulating doctrine and taking swift, harsh action. It was at this point that the Roman Catholic Church formalized much of its doctrine through a series of councils, developing catechisms, and mobilized a movement to defend and propagate what it held as the only true faith. Nothing better captures the essence of the Counter-Reformation than the founding and rapid rise of the Society of Jesus, the Jesuit order.

The Jesuits were founded in 1534 by Ignatius of Loyola, a Spanish noble. A soldier by trade, Ignatius had been wounded in battle and, during his recovery, had devoted himself to the study of religious material. As he studied, he experienced a great enlightening, which led him to retire from his life as a noble soldier to become a lowly hermit. In these early years of heightened religious fervor, he wrote what would eventually become the guidebook for every Jesuit: *The Spiritual Exercises*. By the early 1530s he had traveled to Paris to study at the university, and he arrived during a time of religious turmoil—the very time when John Calvin was leaving Paris

Stephen and me standing on a castle wall, high above a pass in Italy
© Stephen McCaskell

fleeing for his life. In 1540 Pope Paul III first recognized the newly founded Society of Jesus, and Ignatius was its first superior general.[1]

The Jesuits were distinguished from other monastic orders by their zealous, sworn obedience to the pope and by their willingness to carry out his every order. They were "to strive especially for the defence and propagation of the faith and for the progress of souls in Christian life and doctrine, by means of public preaching, lectures and any other ministration whatsoever of the Word of God, and further by means of retreats, the education of children and unlettered persons in Christianity, and the spiritual consolation of Christ's faithful."[2] They quickly founded hundreds of educational institutions, became spiritual advisers to great rulers, and sent missionaries all over the world. The Jesuits were primarily responsible for bringing the Catholic faith to Asia, Africa, and the Americas, helping to establish the Roman Catholic Church as a truly global faith. They labored hard against the rising growth of the Protestant movement and opposed their "seditious" theology. Nick Needham draws an interesting comparison: "If Luther gave birth to Protestantism, Loyola was the spiritual father of Counter-Reformation Catholicism."[3]

I wanted to learn more about the Jesuits, so I visited the "mother church" of the order, Rome's Chiesa del Santissimo Nome di Gesù (which, thankfully, is abbreviated to Chiesa del Gesù or "Church of Jesus"). I found several objects that powerfully display what the Jesuits stood for and what they believed God had called them to do, both in the church building and in the attached museum. The church houses a particularly strange and macabre object that I was eager to see, but on my visit I was surprised to find something even more vivid that captured my interest.

Traditional Roman Catholic churches and cathedrals tend to be constructed in the shape of a cross, and Chiesa del Gesù is no exception. The nave, or shaft of the cross, runs the length of the building and features a magnificently frescoed ceiling far overhead. In each of the transepts (arms of the cross) is a smaller chapel, one dedicated to the founder of the order and one to his foremost disciple. On the right is the Chapel of St. Francis Xavier. It features a towering painting of the saint's death, though the detail is difficult to make out unless you happen to visit when the light is just right. Between that painting above and an ornate gold altar below, is a silver reliquary that displays the left forearm of St. Francis Xavier. Yes, his left forearm. This arm is said to have baptized three hundred thousand people and is now considered a relic worthy of veneration. As I sat in the chapel for a time, I saw many of the faithful make a financial donation, light a candle, genuflect before it, and

seek the saint's intercession. A pilgrim from India asked me to take his photo with the arm in the background. He explained excitedly that he had already seen the rest of Xavier's body in Goa, India, and was feeling greatly blessed that he had now seen the whole thing.

I turned around and saw another altar in the left chapel, with large sculptures on both sides. This is the Chapel of St. Ignatius of Loyola and, like its counterpart, features a great painting. The saint's body is entombed beneath the altar, but the two sculptures are what arrested my attention. The one to the left is *The Triumph of Faith over Idolatry*, a work by Jean-Baptiste Théodon. Here a barbarian king and peasant woman are being trodden upon by a woman

The Triumph of Faith over Heresy

LUTHER GETS CRUSHED

Another interesting sculpture is in the nearby Chiesa di Sant'Ignazio di Loyola, or Church of St. Ignatius of Loyola. In the left transept, you'll find a statue of Loyola stepping on the neck of Martin Luther. This is yet another sign of the Jesuits' mission to triumph over the Protestant heresy.

who represents the true church or the true faith. She holds a golden chalice high in the air while the king and peasant lie at her feet, looking up at her in awe and terror. With her left foot she crushes the neck of a terrible dragon, and in this vivid image we see the triumph of the Roman Catholic Church over idolatrous kings and commoners. The church, after all, claimed supremacy over all humanity with its pope as Pontifex Maximus.

To the right side of the altar is a second sculpture, this one the work of Pietro Le Gros and titled *The Triumph of Faith over Heresy*. Here that same woman holds a flame in one hand and a cross in the other. Two men cry out in fear and agony as they tumble toward hell and damnation. A vicious serpent and a pair of books fall with them, while nearby an angel tears pages out of another volume. Fascinated, I wondered, *Who are these people and what are the books?* My later research revealed that it is surprisingly difficult to find an authoritative answer, but I believe the sculpture itself gave me the clues I needed to answer definitively. Because the interior of the building is dim, it can

be difficult to make out every detail, but I happened to bring a light and tried to shine it on the darkest parts of the sculpture. As I did so, I noticed some small but crucial details. On the spine of one book is the name "Mart Luther," and on the other "Joann Calvin." It was only after I returned home and more closely studied the photographs I had taken that I saw some lettering on the spine of the book being torn apart by the angel: "Hulderic Zwingli." Luther, Calvin, and Zwingli were three of the most influential leaders of the Protestant Reformation, and clearly they were viewed as the archenemies of the Roman Catholic Church.

Here in *The Triumph of Faith over Heresy*, a prominent sculpture within the mother church of the Jesuit order, we see the Roman Catholic Church triumphing over the Protestant heresy. Or, if we look at it from a Protestant perspective, we see the Catholic Church mobilizing and militarizing her followers to counter and even persecute those who preach the gospel of grace alone through faith alone. The Jesuits were organized like an army, with their priests known as "God's Soldiers" following directions under their "superior general." Through their zealotry and absolute loyalty to their faith and their pope, they brought great suffering to many of God's people. In some nations they managed to virtually snuff out the rising Protestant movement, while in others they would prove to be a fearsome and persuasive opponent.[4]

By studying the sculpture and hearing the story it tells, I was able to learn how the established church responded to this most significant challenge. The Reformation continued to spread, but its leaders and followers faced increasing opposition. Meanwhile, the Council of Trent formalized the doctrine of the Roman Catholic Church in opposition to Protestantism, declaring anathemas, or curses, against anyone who failed to hold the views taught by Rome. The church used its excommunicating power

to intimidate rulers and commoners alike into subservience. It instituted the Inquisition to terrify and torture those who threatened to defect. And it used its new army of obedient priests to persuade and enforce. *The Triumph of Faith over Heresy*, though created after these years, remains a vivid representation of the purpose, the history, and the ultimate goals of the Society of Jesus. Beyond that, it remains a vivid reminder that the Roman Catholic Church has never retracted the anathemas of the Council of Trent and that it continues to teach a gospel that adds the necessity of human merit to the giving of God's free grace.

For the next object, I would travel back to England to see how the Roman Catholic Church dealt with another man it deemed a heretic to its cause.

13
THOMAS CRANMER'S SHACKLE

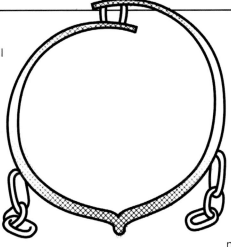

Any survey of history will turn up some periods that are fascinating to study, but personally I find the period of Tudor rule in England especially interesting. From 1485 to 1603 England went through a series of events that transformed the nation from a country wholly in the grasp of the Roman Catholic Church to a nation fully freed from its control, from a nation where the ruler had to be Roman Catholic to a nation where the ruler was forbidden to be Roman Catholic. This was a time marked by the strong rule of Henry VIII and his daughter Elizabeth I, with two other family members (and one distant relation) ruling briefly between the two. It was an era of glorious triumphs on the battlefields and bloody persecutions in the prisons. It was a time that led to consequential change in England, charting a new path for the nation and the world dominated by the emerging British Empire.

The story of the Tudors cannot be fully understood apart from the name of Thomas Cranmer, the archbishop of Canterbury. Through the long, seminal reign of Henry VIII, no adviser was more trusted and constant for the king than Cranmer. Cranmer used his position to reform the church, yet his reforms could go no further than Henry's eclectic brand of Christianity, which embraced a mixture of both Protestant and Catholic principles. Through the short reign of Edward VI, Henry's son, who leaned strongly Protestant, Cranmer was able to implement his reforms to a far greater degree than he had under Henry. But then, under the cruel reign of Mary I, a staunch Catholic, he paid the ultimate price. I had a lead on an object in Oxford's Ashmolean Museum and was eager to track it down so I could learn the story it tells about Cranmer and the English Reformation.

Thomas Cranmer was born in Aslockton, England, in 1489 and trained for the priesthood as a young man. He came to the attention of King Henry VIII when Henry was searching for a way to dissolve his marriage to Catherine of Aragon so he could instead marry Anne Boleyn. While most clergymen outright refused to give any consideration to the idea of a divorce, Cranmer suggested it should become a matter of discussion at the universities. Delighted, Henry made Cranmer his chaplain and later the archbishop of Canterbury, the foremost position in the English church. With Cranmer's support, Henry was able to secure his divorce and marry Anne Boleyn, though he would soon find a way out of that marriage as well.[1]

At some point in his studies, Cranmer encountered Reformation theology and began to be persuaded by it. Although he always remained committed to doing the bidding of his king, and though his beliefs never quite equaled those of some of the leading continental Reformers, his Protestant convictions grew and deepened through his lifetime, as did his confidence in the Bible and his desire to see it widely distributed across the nation.[2] During the short reign of the precociously godly Edward VI, Cranmer produced the Book of Common Prayer and the Forty-Two Articles, which, more than any other documents, described and defined the worship and theology of the Church of England.[3]

Edward VI's rule was short-lived, as he died at just fifteen years of age, and Mary, his earnestly Catholic older sister, seized the throne. She immediately began to suppress Protestantism and advocated for a return to Catholicism. Leading Protestants like Hugh Latimer and Nicholas Ridley were imprisoned in Oxford's Bocardo Prison and charged with acts of treason and heresy. They were soon joined by Thomas Cranmer, where he awaited his own trial. To guard against any chance of escape, he was fastened to the wall by an iron band.

Oxford's Ashmolean Museum, just a short walk from the site of the prison, houses a tiny exhibit dedicated to the men who would come to be known as the Oxford Martyrs. The museum exhibit displays the key that locked the doors of the prison until it was torn down

Thomas Cranmer's shackle

Here are some other things to see in Oxford:

- The Martyrs' Memorial at the strange intersection of St. Giles', Magdalen Street, and Beaumont Street commemorates the Oxford Martyrs.
- The Martyr's Mark is the actual spot in which the Oxford Martyrs were executed. There is a spot in the roadway and a plaque on a nearby building.
- The Eagle and Child is a pub where C. S. Lewis, J. R. R. Tolkien, and the rest of the "Inklings" used to meet. It remains open for business.

in 1771, and next to the key is the iron band that held Cranmer. It is a great hinged shackle that could be fastened around a prisoner and then be held closed by a lock. Two chains run from it and would have once been fastened to a wall to keep the prisoner confined. It is rugged in appearance, austere and intimidating. Although it is now pitted with age, it is not difficult to imagine the discomfort it once brought and the sense of hopelessness it provoked.

Latimer and Ridley were burned at the stake on October 16, 1555, and their friend Cranmer was forced to watch the gruesome scene. It appears that the misery of prison, the psychological pressure of his examiners, the trauma of watching these excruciating deaths, and the heavy chains around his body caused him to waver in his faith, and on a number of occasions he recanted his Protestant positions. Nevertheless, he was still sentenced to death, and before he went to the stake he recanted his recantations and repented of wavering. John Foxe recounted his final moments:[4] "When the wood was kindled, and the fire began to burn near him, stretching out his arm, he put his right hand into the flame, which he held so steadfast and immovable (saving that once with the same hand he wiped his face), that all men might see his hand burned before his body was touched."[5] He allowed his right hand to burn first as a sign of his repentance, for it was with his right hand that he had signed those recantations. He was the third and last of the Oxford Martyrs who are now commemorated in a large memorial at the intersection of St. Giles', Beaumont Street, and Magdalen Street. Yet these three men were just a few of the hundreds of Protestants who would lose their lives under the reign of "Bloody Mary." Thankfully, Mary's reign did not last, and neither did the time of persecution. Soon Henry's younger daughter, Elizabeth, gained the throne and brought stability to the nation, renewing and strengthening the Protestant position of the Church of England.

The Reformation continued to develop and thrive in England. In fact, for a time England became the center of Protestant faith and missions as it carried Reformation doctrines across the globe through commerce and exploration. The English Reformation encompassed many of the writers of the Puritan movement, leading to the preachers of the Great Awakening, and numerous men and women who went abroad as part of the modern missions movement. These later works were built on the tireless labors and ultimate sacrifices of Christian leaders like Thomas Cranmer. As I studied that cold, iron shackle, I could see a key point in the flow of history. In the life and death of Cranmer, I witnessed Henry's break with Rome, Edward's promising but too-short reign, Mary's bloody rule, and Elizabeth's establishment of a new order. And above all, I saw the providence of God in creating a context in which his gospel could thrive and its influence expand. The Lord so often works in mysterious ways.

I would see that theme again as I returned north again to Scotland.

14

ST. GILES' PULPIT

As Protestantism's teachings continued to spread, new approaches to worship developed. Whereas Roman Catholic worship was centered on the celebration of the Eucharist on the altar, Protestant worship was centered on the preaching of the Word from the pulpit. It is impossible to imagine the recovery of biblical doctrine without the recovery of biblical preaching. While the Reformation was spread through books and tracts and personal conversation, its foremost medium was preaching. And I was able to listen to this historical development and see it reflected in the Reformed Church gallery of the National Museum of Scotland.

It did not take long for Reformation doctrine to make the short voyage from continental Europe to Scotland. By the early 1520s, traders from the Netherlands were carrying Lutheran writings and convictions to Scottish ports, and these teachings quickly took root in coastal cities like Edinburgh and St. Andrews. At this time Scotland was firmly in the grip of Roman Catholic monarchs who were guided by powerful church leaders. Patrick Hamilton, a twenty-four-year-old leading Protestant preacher became Scotland's first Protestant martyr when he was captured, tried, and burned at the stake in 1528.[1]

As the power and popularity of the Reformation expanded, Scotland found itself pressed between Protestant England and Catholic France, though the marriage of Scotland's James V to France's Mary of Guise showed that Scottish leaders intended to remain Catholic, loyal to the pope. Still, it was impossible to stop the spread of Protestant doctrine throughout Scotland, and by the late 1530s, a Catholic leader, Cardinal Beaton, initiated a large-scale effort to suppress and destroy Scottish Protestantism once and for all.

It was in this context that George Wishart rose as Scotland's next great Protestant preacher. Wishart traveled throughout the Scottish lowlands preaching the Bible and seeing many come to Christ. He traveled with a bodyguard named John Knox, but despite their efforts, neither Knox nor his associates were able to stop Beaton from tracking down and executing Wishart.[2] We know very little of Knox's early years, and little more of his conversion or his time with Wishart. But we do know that he was captured by the French in 1547 and spent at least two years in hard labor as a galley slave. The years following his release were a time of turbulence during which he spent time as a preacher at several locations in England, Scotland, and the Continent. Although his return to Scotland was brief and interrupted by persecution, it was long enough and its impact felt strongly enough to make him a popular hero among his countrymen.[3] He spent several years in Geneva, ministering alongside John Calvin, who was a key influence on him. By 1559 the situation in Scotland had sufficiently stabilized that he could return and take up a preaching ministry in his homeland. This time he decided to focus his efforts at Scotland's most important church in its most important city—St. Giles' Cathedral in Edinburgh.

Today St. Giles' remains open to the public, and it begs a visit. I couldn't help but note the irony of seeing a sculpture of Knox (who was adamantly opposed to images) standing within the church where he once ministered. Strangely, Knox's grave is in the parking lot outside, a simple marker under a parked car noting the place where his body was laid. Knox's house is a short walk down the Royal Mile and has been turned into a museum. But St. Giles' was not my primary destination. I knew that my visit to Edinburgh wouldn't be complete without a stop at the nearby National Museum of Scotland. This museum houses a vast collection of objects spanning Scotland's prehistory to modern times. It has a large and diverse collection of artifacts related to the Reformation. On display is Alexander Peden's mask, a bizarre and

St. Giles' Cathedral, Edinburgh, Scotland

pxhere.com, Creative Commons CC0

haunting reminder of the days when Protestants were persecuted. Near the mask is a copy of the National Covenant, a document that would become an important part of Scottish history, written a generation after Knox lived and died. Between these two objects, planted on the floor, is the pulpit that once stood in St. Giles' Cathedral.

In Scotland, perhaps more than anywhere else in the world at that time, the Reformation was led by preaching. It began in the pulpit and spread from there. Reformation doctrine revealed a deep hunger for the Word of God that could be satisfied only by the faithful preaching of the Word. And week after week, as Knox thundered from his pulpit, he satisfied the hunger of his people. Knox's preaching was fearless, powerful, and effective, and through it many Scots heard the gospel and turned to Christ in repentance and faith. He insisted he had been "called to instruct the ignorant, comfort the sorrowful, confirm the weak, and rebuke the proud."[4] Following Knox's example, countless other preachers took up the task until there was an undeniable movement of God across the land.

Knox's pulpit in St. Giles' was long ago replaced by a much grander one, so the original

Standing before the statue of John Knox in St. Giles' Cathedral
© Stephen McCaskell

now stands here, in the National Museum of Scotland.[5] Darkened by age and worn by use, it is remarkably plain, as if to suggest that the physical pulpit itself has no bearing on the power of the words that come from it. In that way it contrasts so nicely with many of the grand and ornate pulpits constructed since the time of the Reformation. This unadorned little frame simply elevated the man so he could be seen and heard as he brought the Word of God to the people of God.

This pulpit—and, indeed, the story of the Scottish Reformation—reminded and assured me that God consistently works through the preaching of his Word. What seems foolishness to the world (and, sadly, to many Christians as well) is powerful and effective, the means God has appointed for both salvation and sanctification, for rescuing his people *and* calling them to lives consecrated to his service.

As Paul said, "For since in the wisdom of God the world through its wisdom did not know him, God was pleased through the foolishness of what was preached to save those who believe" (1 Corinthians 1:21). Knox's pulpit stands as a reminder that great movements of God begin with the simple preaching of the Word. It stands as a challenge that we must trust in the power of the preached Word and not the flair of the preacher. And as I studied it, I felt this pulpit serving as a warning as well, for just as Scotland was once sparked to life by the rise of preaching, the flames of spiritual fervor have now faded, and today Scotland is once again a nation in desperate need of revival. May God raise up a new generation who follow in the steps of John Knox!

My next journey was the longest of all, and it would take me to the opposite side of the world from my home.

15

KING JAMES BIBLE

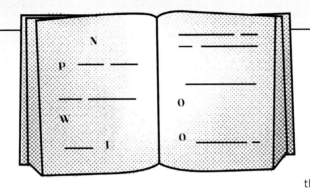

A funny thing happens when you fly from Canada to Australia. A day disappears along the way. I left Toronto on a Tuesday and arrived on Thursday. Wednesday evaporated somewhere far over the Pacific as I crossed the International Date Line. There were a few times on my journey when I was tempted to complain and gripe about the length of the flight and the discomfort of sitting in a small space. But then I was reminded of the nearly fourteen hundred people who had made the inaugural journey to Australia some 230 years before. Their journey was far longer—and far more dangerous.

I was traveling to Australia looking for Bibles, of all things. In particular I went looking for a copy of the most important book in the history of the English language: the King James Bible. The work on the King James Bible had been sponsored by King James VI of Scotland who, upon the death of Elizabeth I, also become James I, king of England. At that time there were at least two prominent English translations, but one, the Bishop's Bible, was substandard, and the other, the Geneva Bible, had marginal notes that were considered anti-monarchy. James decided to convene a committee that would create a new, superior, authorized translation.[1]

James's committee of nearly fifty scholars began meeting in 1604. By 1611 they had finished, and the first of their newly translated Bibles came off the presses to great acclaim. A work of excellent scholarship and tremendous linguistic beauty, the Authorized Version, soon to be widely known as the King James Version, became *the* Bible of the English language. It would retain that status for centuries.[2]

Somehow, a first printing of the first edition—one of only two hundred copies known to exist—has ended up more than ten thousand miles from England in the library of Sydney's Moore College, where it forms part of their Treasures collection. Having flown for

HOW TO TOUCH AN OLD BOOK

In my journey I had the opportunity to touch and even hold some ancient and valuable books, letters, and manuscripts. I had expected I'd be required to wear gloves while doing so, but learned there are now two schools of thought on that. Some people believe it is best to wear gloves to protect against the oils on our skin. Others believe the gloves deaden our touch and make us handle the objects too roughly. Those people believe that the oils are the lesser of two evils. I learned that it is important to ask.

twenty-two hours, I was eager to get off the plane and go exploring. I made the college my first stop. I found this edition of the Bible to be a beautiful old book, though it is showing evidence of its age. I gingerly turned its crackling pages to locate Ruth chapter 3, where I could verify a well-known typo that is characteristic of the first printing of the first edition. What a thrill it was to hold such a rare, important, and valuable Bible!

Not far from Moore College I was able to view yet another King James Bible, one that was even more intriguing to me (though it wasn't quite as ancient). This second Bible is significant because it's a King James Bible, but also because it played a unique role in the founding of Australia and in telling how the Christian faith first arrived on its shores. I listened to its story (by listening to Justin Moffatt, one of the pastors of Church Hill Anglican, who kindly gave me an hour of his time), and learned I'd need to advance in history just a little bit.

The famous Captain James Cook discov-

ered Australia during his Pacific voyage of 1770. Landing near modern-day Sydney, he claimed the land for the British Crown and gave it the name New South Wales. After claiming it, he left to report its existence and distinguishing features to the English authorities. Someone saw unusual potential for using the land. The English at that time had a practice of sending their convicts to overseas penal colonies. Until then, their favored spot to send convicts had been the Americas. But after 1776 and American independence, the colonies were no longer interested in taking convicts from other nations. The English needed an alternative.[3] They decided that Australia would make an ideal location and formed the First Fleet under the leadership of Commodore Arthur Phillip to set sail and establish a new penal colony. The fleet of eleven ships carried around fourteen hundred sailors, soldiers, convicts, and free citizens when it set sail from Portsmouth on May 13, 1787. Incredibly, all eleven ships survived the long voyage and arrived eight months later,

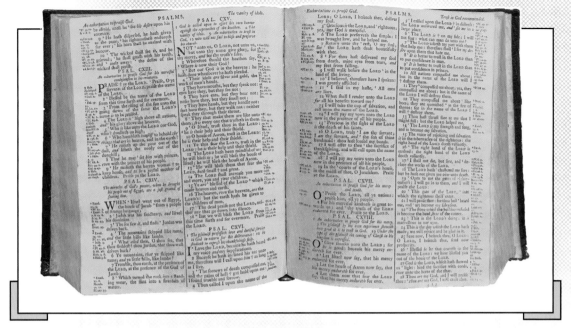

The Fleet Bible

a few ships at a time, between January 18 and 20, 1788. On January 26 the fleet sailed into Port Jackson, and Phillip and several others went ashore at Sydney Cove to raise the British flag, formally claiming the land. Australia had been founded.[4]

The fleet, while largely made up of soldiers, sailors, and settlers, also had a chaplain. While many people in England saw the new colony as an opportunity to increase the wealth and glory of the empire, others saw it as a unique opportunity for Christian ministry. This was the burden of the Eclectic Society, which counted among its members the hymn writer John Newton and the politician William Wilberforce, both of whom we will run into again before long. This society was convinced that the new colony could thrive only if it had a chaplain to promote

morality, preach the gospel to the unconverted, and tend to the spiritual needs of the people. They proposed to send Richard Johnson, and he was accepted for the position. Johnson was provided with a huge supply of books and other teaching material and sent on his way.[5]

The first Sunday after the fleet landed was February 3, 1788, and Richard Johnson stood on Australian soil and preached the very first sermon in the new nation's history, taking as his text Psalm 116:12: "What shall I render unto the LORD for all his benefits toward me?" (KJV). He preached that day from a King James Bible, a copy that has survived through the centuries. Now known as the Fleet Bible, it is housed at Church Hill Anglican Church, though it is only occasionally on public display. In the early 1900s a tradition began in which every member of the British royal family visiting Sydney signed the Bible. Beginning with Edward VIII, it has since been signed by George VI and his wife Elizabeth; by Queen Elizabeth II and Prince Philip; by Prince Charles and Princess Diana; by Andrew and Sarah, Duke and Duchess of York; and most recently, by William and Kate, the Duke and Duchess of Cambridge. It was a joy to turn the pages of the Bible to Psalm 116, to read its words, and to consider the important role this Bible has played in the history of a great nation.

In its own way, the Fleet Bible reminded me of the lasting impact and longevity of the King James Bible, for this translation has been present at the founding of great nations and the funerals of forgotten believers. It has been laid on the pulpits at the coronation ceremonies of kings and queens and on the pulpits of tiny churches in forgotten corners of the world. It has been present for the oaths of office for renowned presidents and prime ministers and for the personal devotions of millions of unknown saints. I could not understand the history of our world, much less the history of the Christian faith, without accounting for it.

Long before Australia was settled by the British, several European nations had founded colonies in the New World, the Americas. In fact, there's an interesting link between American independence and the first Australian settlers. My next destination would allow me to explore the founding of America.

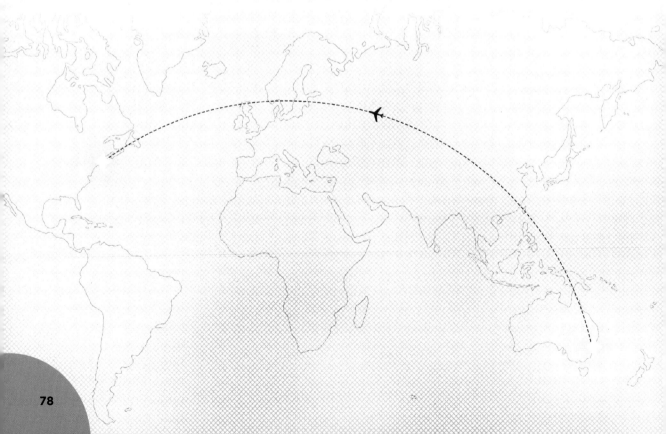

DEFILED TONGAN IDOLS

Because I was already in Australia, I decided to make the short hop to New Zealand to research how the gospel had reached that land. I visited the Auckland War Memorial Museum, which, despite its name, contains exhibits on a wide range of topics. During my visit I was captivated by a pair of wooden idols from the Pacific island of Tonga that tell us an amazing story.

Missionaries had to make several attempts to establish a foothold on Tonga, but when they did, the gospel spread quickly, leading to a powerful movement of the people embracing

This beautiful waterfall was one of many I saw in New Zealand.

Christianity. One of the first of the islanders to convert was a man named Taufaʻahau (who later became King George Tupou I). He accepted Christ in 1831 after being discipled by Wesleyan missionaries. As he began to hear the gospel and to grapple with its claims, he grew disillusioned with his traditional gods and put them to the test. When they failed him, his skepticism grew until he finally embraced the Christian God.

In the diary of missionary John Williams, we read about Taufaʻahau and his new faith. Taufaʻahau "drove a large herd of pigs into the sacred enclosure . . . and suspended the gods by the neck to the rafters of the house in which they had been adored! . . . On observing five goddesses hanging by the neck, I requested this intrepid chief to give me one of them, which he immediately cut down and presented to me."[1]

One of those "goddesses" was given to the missionary and eventually made its way to this museum in New Zealand where it remains on display. Made of extremely hard wood, the body of the goddess Hikuleʻo is angular, her face triangular, her long arms descending to a point, her legs stooped, her large breasts jutting far outward. Notably, she bears a number of indentations and scratches—perhaps a sign that she has been beaten and trampled on.[2] The marks on the idol of this goddess tell us a story of a leader who embraced the gospel and led his people away from their false gods toward the one true God. It's a story that is familiar because it is repeated again and again throughout the spread of Christianity.

16

WILLIAM BREWSTER'S CHEST

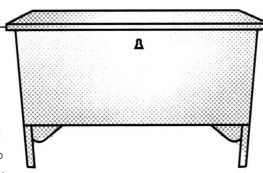

My expansive study of Christian history helped me see how the "center" of Christian geography has shifted from time to time. As the strength and influence of Christianity declines in one area, it inevitably rises in another. In its early days, the Christian faith was centered in Jerusalem, but that center soon shifted to Rome and then Constantinople. The early Reformation era saw further shifts with the rise of the Protestant movement and the establishment of the church in Germany, Switzerland, and the Netherlands as the home of many prominent Protestants. As the Reformation progressed, there was soon a further shift to England, and eventually America took its turn. Today we see what may be the beginning of a new shift toward the global south.

For the next object, I wanted to better understand one of the more recent shifts—the shift from England to America. (It's worth remembering that though this shift may seem to be far in the past, it actually happened at the three-quarter mark of church history as we know it.) How did the gospel first arrive in America? To learn more of this history, I visited Pilgrim Hall in Plymouth, Massachusetts, where I was able to see a wonderful collection of objects related to some of America's first and best-known Christians.

The fifteenth and sixteenth centuries brought new shipbuilding techniques, enabling ships to go faster and farther than ever before. Meanwhile, navigation methods advanced so that ships could carry explorers across distant oceans. With the blessing and sponsorship of the Spanish monarchy, Christopher Columbus sailed west from Spain and, over a succession of voyages, discovered the Caribbean islands, Central America, and South America. These discoveries marked the start of an age of exploration and conquest in which many European

This was taken at a beach outside of Plymouth.

© Aileen Challies

powers laid claim to large portions of the New World. Each country took their faith with them—the French, Spanish, and Portuguese brought their Catholicism, while the English and Dutch brought their Protestantism. Among the first English settlers to make the perilous voyage and to undertake the difficult task of settling a new land was a man named William Brewster.

We know very few details of Brewster's early life, except that he was born around 1567, probably in Nottinghamshire, England. As a young man, he served in various clerical positions for leaders in both the church and government. By the early 1600s, he had married and had a family. Importantly, he had also adopted separatist views, the belief that the Church of England had become so corrupt that faithful Christians must now separate from it. His friend

William Bradford later wrote that Brewster had been faithful in serving separatist believers and congregations, even hosting a church in his home for a time.[1] In 1607 a time of persecution against the separatists compelled Brewster and several others to flee to Holland where they could worship in peace. But ten years later Brewster was back in England, attempting to organize a move to the newly established American colonies. Although the task was difficult, he persevered, and finally he, his family, and several others set sail on a ship called the *Mayflower* on September 6, 1620.

Although they had intended to settle in the existing Jamestown colony, they were blown off course and landed in modern-day Massachusetts. After sighting land on November 9, they anchored near Cape Cod on November

William Brewster's Chest

Pilgrim Hall Museum, Plymouth, MA

11, where they prepared and signed a document called the Mayflower Compact, establishing the governance of a new colony. After exploring the nearby coastline, they settled in Plymouth, where a monument at Plymouth Rock now marks the traditional landing spot. In the new settlement, Brewster took on the role of the settlers' pastor and spiritual leader.[2] Although he remained a separatist, he maintained a conciliatory tone toward other church and government leaders, working closely with Bradford, who served as the first governor. As one of his biographers writes, "He alone held the Pilgrim church together during the early years of settlement, maintaining both its orthodoxy and its willingness to interact with nonseparating Puritans."[3] The Pilgrim settlers would need to maintain peaceful relationships with others, for

the early years were full of terrible difficulties. Still, the colony survived and grew, gaining a significant foothold on the new continent.

Today Pilgrim Hall in Plymouth, Massachusetts, maintains an extensive collection of those first settlers' possessions. The day I visited was unusually warm for February, though freezing rain was in the forecast despite the warmer temperatures. I learned that the collection of objects was in the basement of the hall, and proceeded downstairs. In a case near the entrance to the exhibit is William Bradford's Geneva Bible, a psalter, the only portrait of one of the pilgrims that was painted from life, and several household items and pieces of furniture. Most of the items that were carried on the *Mayflower* were extremely practical, as there was little room for luxuries—the museum holds an ironware pot, for example, and a wicker cradle. But what drew my attention, for some reason, was William Brewster's chest. Brewster carried this Dutch-made chest first from Holland to England, then from England to America. It stands just over two feet high, is nearly four feet wide, and still bears its original ochre paint. Its edges are reinforced by a number of iron straps, and its hinges are hidden inside. It is, in almost every way, unremarkable to the eye. Although it may have some value and interest for its age, its provenance is what makes it such an important object. Of all the possessions an early settler could bring with him, nothing was more important than a chest, since it served as both storage and seating along the way and at his final destination. It's such a simple object and so mundane. But it seems to tell the story of leaving one land and going to another, and doing so for the sake of religious conviction. Brewster and the other Pilgrims couldn't have known they would settle a land that, for many years, would be a bastion of freedom where the gospel could thrive.

Persecution first prompted these faithful men and women to flee to the New World. They carried with them little more than the simplest and barest necessities, and this unremarkable chest is among their most precious remains. It told me that Brewster's arrival—like his chest—was rather inauspicious. Few would have known that at the start of this new settlement those Pilgrims carried something of infinite prominence and worth—the gospel of Jesus Christ. They founded their new colony as a place where they and others could worship God in freedom of conscience, and though it may be difficult to argue that America is or was a truly Christian nation, it was certainly a nation founded on Christian principles, fertile ground for the gospel to take deep root. In the years to come, the American colonies and the new nation formed from them would become the setting for the Lord to continue his work in remarkable ways. There would be more to see and tell in America, but first I needed to reverse Brewster's route and return to England to visit the home of one of the bestselling authors of all time.

17

JOHN BUNYAN'S JUG

Recent years have seen an unexpected resurgence of interest in the Puritans. The interest can be traced to the writings and influence of theologians like J. I. Packer, who made no secret of his own indebtedness to Puritan authors, and to preachers like Martyn Lloyd-Jones, who demonstrated the richness of Puritan thought in his preaching and writing. Publishers like Banner of Truth and Reformation Heritage Books have made the very best Puritan literature accessible and affordable. These efforts have led to a contemporary rediscovery of some of the great theological and devotional treasures of the past.

Yet there is one Puritan writer who has always been known, and whose impact and popularity has rarely waned, and I will allow him to represent them all. Although John Bunyan authored many works during his lifetime, his book *The Pilgrim's Progress from This World to That Which Is to Come*, or more simply, *The Pilgrim's Progress*, has firmly established his place in history. First published in 1678, *The Pilgrim's Progress* has since been translated into more than two hundred languages and bears the distinction of never having gone out of print. It is considered the first novel in the English language and is one of the bestselling and most read books of all time. There was a time when this book was found alongside the Bible in virtually every respectable English home.[1]

My journey to listen to the epic history of the Christian faith took me, unsurprisingly, to the John Bunyan Museum in Bedford, England, where I found a plain little object that played a surprising role in the life of this great Puritan. Puritanism, in Bunyan's day, was a reform movement with the goal of divesting the Church of England of any last traces of Catholicism while more positively focusing Christian life and worship on Scripture as the basis for doctrine and practice.[2] Although the term *Puritan* was originally used in a pejorative sense, it aptly described those who were concerned for the purity of Christ's

This is the oldest remaining Baptist church in England.

church. Some of these Puritans remained within the established church, while others were driven out by conscience or necessity. Altogether they created a massive body of sermons, books, and other literature that has continued influencing Christians all over the world to this day. But none of the writings have proven as influential as this simple book by Bunyan.

John Bunyan was born in Elstow, Bedford-shire, on November 30, 1628. He was the son of a tinker—a man who repaired pots and pans and other simple household goods—and this is the craft young John would soon take as his own. Despite these simple roots, and despite being a rebellious child who took joy in disobeying God and man, he was educated and learned to read and write, skills that he would later put to good use. John married young, and his first marriage (which would last just a short time before his wife died) brought him four children, including his precious daughter Mary, who was born blind. Now a husband and father, John developed an interest in religion, but he could not find inner peace. One day, while out walking by himself, these words came to his mind: "Thy righteous-ness is in heaven." John suddenly understood that if he was to have any righteousness before God, any place to stand before his Creator, it could not be by his own work or merit but must be because of the righteousness of Christ.[3]

A changed man, John began attending a Separatist church in Bedford, where he quickly progressed and matured in his faith. He began preaching, but he did this at a time when the king was demanding an end to independent preachers. In 1660 Bunyan was arrested for holding a Separatist service and was imprisoned in the county jail. He would remain there for twelve long years. Although his imprisonment was unfair and unjust, it proved to be a time of great literary achievement, for it was during this time that he wrote many of his greatest treasures, including his autobiographical *Grace Abounding to the Chief of Sinners* and his fictional *The Pilgrim's Progress*.

The Pilgrim's Progress is the story of a man named Christian who travels from the City of Destruction to the Celestial City. It is, of course, an allegory—a story in which the main character represents every Christian as we progress from salvation to heaven. As he journeys, Christian meets a host of characters who represent different supports and temptations, and he encounters many dangers and blessings that represent universal aspects of human experience. In this way the book is both theological and devotional, fiction and fact. It is packed full of profound insights and has been a great comfort and challenge to generations of Christians, myself included.

Although the Bedford Jail where Bunyan was held no longer stands, a plaque on the bustling street corner is inscribed, "On this site

John Bunyan's jug

stood the Bedford county gaol where John Bunyan was imprisoned for twelve years 1660–1672." Just a short walk away is the John Bunyan Museum, which holds several interesting objects, including the anvil Bunyan used as a tinker, a handmade wooden flute he played during his long imprisonment, and the church minute book that records his death in 1688. But among all of these objects, it was a simple stoneware jug that caught my attention. It seemed to powerfully capture something of his life and influence, and I felt it had a story to tell me.

Although Bunyan loved all his children, he had a special affection for his blind daughter Mary, "who lay nearer my heart than all I had besides."[4] The thought that he might die and leave Mary and the rest of the family destitute caused him great anguish. He longed to be a free man yet also knew he must heed his conscience and so continued his refusal to recant. And it was through this suffering, not apart from it, that he was able to write his greatest works.

In the providence of God, Bunyan would change the world and challenge generations of Christians, and he would do this from a cold and uncomfortable prison, and Mary would play an unexpectedly important role in the writing of her father's greatest work. Historians have speculated that the vividness of the settings, characters, and action in *The Pilgrim's Progress* is Bunyan's way of ensuring the book would appeal even to his blind daughter. She could not see, so he would be her eyes. She must rely on her imagination, so he would feed it with riveting scenes and exciting characters. And that wasn't her only contribution. As her father languished in prison, Mary made daily treks to visit and to bring him his food. Tradition records that day after day she would dutifully carry a small jug from home to the jail.[5]

Although the jug is a simple and plain object, nothing more than a small soup container with a zigzag pattern, it is at the same time one of the most vivid objects in the museum. It tells a great story. Through it I could better understand the dogged resolve of the Puritans and their determination to purify the church—not through violence or warfare but through the faithful study and careful application of Scripture. Through this jug I caught a glimpse of their willingness to suffer for their convictions. And through it I sensed their deep commitment to godliness, a commitment that reaches through the ages to touch me today, to make me want to learn from them and, in so many ways, to be like them.

The next object would take me from England to France, and there I would encounter another person who suffered deeply, though where Bunyan's story has been told and retold through the centuries, hers has mostly been forgotten.

18
MARIE DURAND'S INSCRIPTION

REGISTER

The history of the Christian faith is a story of great joys mixed with deep sorrows. Because the gospel's greatest advances often are met with the greatest suffering, it's also a story of God sovereignly using suffering for his purposes and for the advance of his mission. As I traveled the world, I saw this truth in an unexpected place and time, one that many have forgotten today. It was a story about the Huguenots of France, those Reformation-era Protestants who suffered so deeply yet left such a deep impression on France and the rest of the world.

France has several museums and sites dedicated to the Huguenots and to the "wilderness period" when they suffered under intense persecution by the Catholic authorities. I visited many of these places and found that they hold fascinating objects—pulpits disguised as casks or barrels, mirrors with hidden compartments for storing forbidden Bibles, and secret hiding spots where pastors and leaders could find refuge from danger. But one object powerfully captured for me both the long-suffering and deep faith of the Huguenots. It is a single word carved into the stone tower of a terrible prison on the Mediterranean coast. Tradition ascribes this carving to a woman named Marie Durand. Her story is as poignant as it is powerful. We do well to recover the memory of it.

Marie's story is best told alongside that of her brother Pierre, for their lives and fates were inextricably intertwined. Both were faithful to their God and both suffered deeply but willingly. Their lives aptly illustrate the Huguenot movement and its impact within France and far beyond.[1] Marie Durand was born to her mother, Claudine, and father, Étienne, in the tiny village of Bouschet de Pranles on July 15, 1711. Her brother, Pierre, had been born eleven years before. Although Marie was baptized Roman

Marie Durand's inscription at the Tower of Constance

Catholic, she was raised Protestant. While she was still a child, her brother began to rise in prominence as a young leader among the Huguenot preachers. He soon began to preach at secret gatherings, and as word got out he was forced into hiding from the Roman Catholic authorities. In 1719 soldiers raided an underground service, and though Pierre escaped, he had no choice but to flee to Switzerland for safety, where he had the privilege of receiving formal theological training. That same year, when Marie was just eight years old, Claudine was found to be hosting Protestant meetings in her home and was arrested. Seven years would pass before the family received any news of

her, and tragically it was the news of her death. Thus, as a young child Marie was permanently separated from her mother and raised primarily by her father.[2]

In 1726 Pierre was ordained as a minister, and he returned to France to preach. Two years later, hoping to catch Pierre, soldiers raided his father's home, where they found a forbidden Bible and psalter. They threatened his father with arrest unless Pierre would agree to permanently leave France, and when Pierre refused his father was sent to Fort Brescou, a terrible island prison off the coast of France. Shortly after this, Marie married Mathieu Serre, but because of their connection to Pierre, both were arrested

There are a number of Huguenot museums in France that are worthy of a visit:

- Musée du Désert in Mialet;
- Musée du Vivarais Protestant (the family home of Marie and Pierre Durand) in Pranles;
- Musée du Protestantisme Dauphinois in Le Poët-Laval; and, of course,
- La Tour de Constance in Aigues Mortes.

and sent to separate prisons. Mathieu was sent to Fort Brescou, and Marie to the Tower of Constance in Aigues-Mortes.

Marie was just eighteen years old when she was confined to that tower. She would be fifty-seven before she was released.[3]

The Tower of Constance had been built almost five hundred years earlier as a military garrison, though today it has been converted to a museum. It is a strange-looking circular stone building rising 130 feet and spanning 70 feet in diameter. Its walls are as much as 20 feet thick and designed to withstand great bombard-ments. By Marie's time it had long been used as a prison. Following the Revocation of the Edict of Nantes, which sanctioned the persecution of Protestants in France, the tower was used primarily to imprison Protestant women.[4] Along with thirty or so other women, Marie was con-fined in the tower, living in barbaric conditions. The guards lived on the ground floor, and the prisoners were above them on the second floor, which was one large, circular room. A hole in the center of the room resembling a well was the means through which the guards would pass up food, water, and other necessities. Apart from that small means of contact, the women were kept in isolation.

Even as they suffered day after day, the women were provided a straightforward path to freedom. All they needed to do to be released was to summon the local priest and speak the words, "I recant." They only needed to deny their Protestant "heresies," embrace the Catholic faith, and they could go free. But Marie steadfastly refused. And this is where it was helpful to make a careful search of the tower. As I looked carefully along the edge of the well in the center of the room, I found a word carved into the stone, a word that has long been attributed to Marie. It is simply the French word *register*, or "resist." It is a word of commitment to the cause of Christ, a word that challenges any who would stand on the edge and consider calling down for the priest. Resist! Resist the temptation to recant. Resist the temptation to compromise and, instead, choose to remain in Christ. For decades Marie resisted, and as she did so, she became a leader among the other women in worship and devotion. For decades she maintained her convictions and remained in that tower.

It was humbling to visit the tower and to consider the appalling conditions these women had endured for so long while reflecting on the power of that single word carved into the stone. The tower and the inscription within it aptly tell the story of the wider Huguenot movement as it stayed steadfast even under great waves of persecution.

Marie's brother, Pierre, was betrayed and arrested in 1732, and he went to his death singing psalms. Although he had pleaded to have his family members released, his request was refused and Marie continued to languish in prison. Ten years later their father, Étienne, was finally released, and though Marie's husband, Mathieu, would also be released seven years later, it was under the condition that he leave France and never return. He and Marie never saw one another again.

In 1767, after almost four decades of living in the tower, Marie and the other prisoners finally received some hope of relief. A local prince had learned of the conditions at the prison, and in shock and horror at what was being done, he ordered the release of its prisoners, even against the wishes of King Louis XV.

The skies could not have been clearer over the Tower of Constance

Marie was finally set free on April 14, 1768, at the age of fifty-seven. She had been in the Tower of Constance for thirty-eight years, and upon release she returned home alone.[5] She died at her home in 1776 at the age of sixty-five, having spent the vast majority of her life in captivity. A decade later Louis XVI would sign the Edict of Toleration, which once again allowed some freedom to France's Protestants, but it was not until the devastating French Revolution that Catholic persecution would end at last, sweeping away the monarchy and finally allowing the free exercise of religion.

Until then God used the Huguenot persecution to spread his gospel in unexpected ways, for over the decades hundreds of thousands of Huguenots were forced to flee France. Wherever they went and settled, they took their Protestant beliefs with them. Colonies settled in the Netherlands, Germany, Switzerland, England, and even Africa and the New World. It is hard to overestimate just how much these Huguenots influenced their new countries and how many came to saving faith under their influence. And, of course, God used the Huguenots to provide many examples of steadfastness in suffering. Some of these believers willingly gave up their lives in obedience to Christ and the gospel, while others, like Marie, gave up their years. Marie entered the tower a fresh-faced young lady and left it a broken old woman, but in all of this she steadfastly resisted and counted it all joy for the name of Christ her Savior. I pray that I would be willing to do the same.

My journey would now take me once again from the Old World to the New World, from France back to America, from a prisoner to a preacher.

19
WHITEFIELD ROCK

If I learned anything from my journey around the world, it's the simple truth that the Lord is *always* at work. Across the earth and over the centuries, he is always working out his purposes through the affairs and decisions of human beings. Something that encouraged me is that he often does this in ways and through people that seem very ordinary. As I studied the history of the church and visited the places where these stories are remembered, I heard countless tales of faithful believers sharing the gospel with their friends and family members and seeing them come to faith. Faithful pastors would preach the Word in little churches, and bit by bit God would draw his people to himself through the gospel of Jesus Christ.

But there are also times when God sees fit to work in extraordinary ways. Sometimes he moves with unusual power and stirs many people in the same place to deep conviction—all at once. These are occasional periods of revival, and this is what we find during the period we now refer to as the Great Awakening. And its story cannot be told apart from the story of George Whitefield.

George Whitefield was born in Gloucester, England, in 1714. His early days were marked by difficulty. George's father died when he was just a young boy, and his mother struggled to make ends meet for the family. Despite these setbacks, George gained an education and was eventually able to attend Oxford, though only by working as a servant for the wealthier students at the school. While at Oxford George made several close friends, and it is not exaggerating to say that these relationships changed his life and, over the coming years, were used by God to forever change history. At Oxford George befriended John and Charles Wesley and joined their Holy Club. Although he was first drawn toward a kind of asceticism, his diligent studies of Scripture and his reading of books like Scougal's *Life of God in the Soul of Man* steered him in a different direction, toward a life of service to others.[1]

Soon after he was ordained by the Church of England, George began to stand out as a preacher of unusual power, and crowds flocked to hear him preach. Many who went to hear him to see what the excitement was about found themselves unexpectedly converted. Yet even as he attracted crowds, many churches were closing their doors to him, concerned about his unorthodox style of preaching and his close ties to the Methodism of the Wesley brothers. Whitefield responded by beginning to preach outdoors and soon found that people by the thousands and tens of thousands would flock to hear him preach God's Word outside, even apart from a church building.[2]

In 1739 Whitefield journeyed to the American South, and then, the following year, he moved north and began to preach in New England. It was here, during his time in New England, that his preaching helped spark what later became known as the Great Awakening. As in England, many churches were unwilling to have him speak, so he took to the fields and the city squares. As he journeyed from the coast to the inland areas, from the great cities to the small villages, people flocked from miles around to hear him. One of the places he stopped to preach was West Brookfield, Massachusetts. There, on October 16, 1739, just a short distance outside the town, he began to preach his message for that day. Although the area was thinly populated, a crowd of four hundred to five hundred people gathered to hear his words.[3] History has not recorded what he preached or how the people responded, but the exact spot where he stood has been remembered and

memorialized. Today you can visit this spot for yourself! It's called Whitefield Rock, and as I plotted my journey through New England, I knew I had to visit it.

Let me offer you some advice if you are considering your own visit. Traveling to New England in February is probably not the wisest idea. The weather can be quite unpredictable, and that was certainly the case when I visited. It was one of the warmest early February days on record, with temperatures soaring to 65 degrees. What was the problem, you might ask? Well, immediately following that unseasonably warm day, there were dire warnings of winter storms and freezing rain. I knew I had enough time to see the site, but I also knew I had to get back to safety before the freezing temperatures would turn the roadways to ice.

For many years the field around Whitefield Rock was open to the public, but the property has recently changed hands, and the new owners use the field to graze cows. They've surrounded it with an electric fence. Thankfully, I was able to get permission to hop the gate and see the rock up close. And, even better, the cows were grazing in a different field that day. I slopped my way through the melting ice and snow and discovered that Whitefield Rock is, as you might suspect, a rock. It's a very large rock and seems out of place amid fields that are otherwise quite flat. Because of its size, it is high enough, large enough, and flat enough that it's not difficult to understand why Whitefield chose it for his platform. I stood beside and on the rock that February day and tried to imagine hundreds of people crowding around it to hear Whitefield preach. Standing there on a quiet winter morning, I could almost hear the echoes of his voice—a voice that historians estimate preached some eighteen thousand sermons and gave another twelve thousand talks and exhortations.[4]

In 1960 the New England Methodist Historical Society mounted a plaque on Whitefield Rock that reads: "George Whitefield, early Methodist evangelist, preached from this rock October 16, 1740, on his first tour of America." That one sermon on that one day was just a small part of a much wider movement of God, one that saw countless numbers of people come to saving faith in Christ Jesus while stirring many more out of their spiritual apathy. Whitefield's visit to New England served as something of a spark, but there were others who played crucial roles as well. In 1741, in nearby Enfield, Connecticut, Jonathan Edwards preached his famous sermon "Sinners in the Hands of an Angry God." Many lesser-known preachers also faithfully exposited the Word and called their listeners to repentance and faith. And, for a time, God worked in extraordinary ways, though by the end of the 1740s the awakening seems to have run its course.

Throughout church history only a few people have had the privilege of preaching the gospel before hundreds or thousands during times of revival, when God has chosen to accomplish his work in extraordinary ways. Whitefield had this calling, a privilege and honor to steward the gospel for his generation.

Whitefield Rock

Most of us will share the gospel in simpler, quieter settings as we reach out to the people God brings into our lives. This is our calling and our privilege. Yet I was compelled, even when doing my utmost to carry out my small part of such a ministry, to commit to pray and call out to God for a new awakening, for a new time when we can see him once again work in those unusual ways. Whitefield Rock, though it is but a slab of stone in an open field, reminded me that God does not need great buildings, the beautiful churches and cathedrals of Christendom. All God needs to carry out his work is a faithful believer who will faithfully preach his gospel.

JONATHAN EDWARDS'S LAZY SUSAN DESK

During my journey through New England, I found an object that wonderfully displays the brilliance and eccentricity of the man who is at once one of America's great philosophers and great theologians (or, if you prefer, philosophical theologians): Jonathan Edwards.

Edwards lived in Stockbridge, Massachusetts, from 1751 to 1758. Historians have long debated why Edwards made this move and what he had hoped to accomplish. Some believe he saw it as a kind of retreat where he could focus on his writing; some believe he wished to serve as a missionary to the frontier. Probably both are true. Whatever the reason, all agree that these years marked the peak of Edwards's writing career.[1] During this time he wrote *Concerning the End for Which God Created the World*, *The Great Christian Doctrine of Original Sin Defended*, and *The Nature of True Virtue*. It was also during this period that he published one of his most enduring classics, *Freedom of the Will*.

In the Stockbridge Library, Museum & Archives is a delightfully quirky object that played an important role in this period of Edwards's life and ministry. In the small local museum housed in the building's basement is a strange, six-sided, wooden desk. Hexagonal in shape, each of the sides is steeply sloped toward a ridge that runs

Jonathan Edwards's eclectic, six-sided lazy Susan desk

along the bottom, and it is clear that each side is meant to hold either a manuscript or an open book. This unique desktop is built on a pillar that allows it to rotate like a lazy Susan.[2] In this odd way, Edwards found a solution to a common problem faced by every author—how to keep many books open and available at one time.

Standing before that desk in that cluttered little museum, it was not difficult to picture Edwards sitting in his study. A manuscript is spread open on his writing desk (now housed at Yale University) with this unique object close beside him. He writes a few sentences, then turns to read from a book that is lying open on one of the six sides. He jots a few words, turns back to the table, and rotates it to yet another book. He studies this one, too, before writing a few more words. And in this way he adds a few more sentences, a few more thoughts, to the classic treatise R. C. Sproul would later describe as "the most important theological work ever produced in America."[3]

20

CHARLES WESLEY'S ORGAN

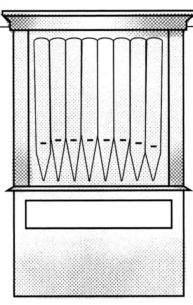

Christians sing. The great truths at the heart of the Christian faith demand to be not merely pondered and spoken but also sung. Throughout history Christian believers have taken seriously the apostle Paul's command to "let the message of Christ dwell among you richly as you teach and admonish one another with all wisdom through psalms, hymns, and songs from the Spirit, singing to God with gratitude in your hearts" (Colossians 3:16). Because Christians *must* sing, Christian hymn writing has a long history.

Arguably the greatest hymn writer in the history of the Christian faith, if only for being the most productive, is Charles Wesley. Charles wrote close to sixty-five hundred hymns in his lifetime, several of which have been translated into multiple languages and many of which are still being sung today. Any survey of favorite hymns is bound to include at least a few of his. Not surprisingly, several museums are dedicated to Charles and his brother John, who were instrumental in the start of the Methodist movement in England during the eighteenth century. The New Room in Bristol is the oldest Methodist chapel in the world, and some of the rooms attached to the chapel once served as John's home. It now houses a museum that tells the story of Methodism, and its archives hold many important books, papers, and manuscripts written by John. Nearby is his brother Charles's home, which contains a few original artifacts from his life and family. But perhaps the most significant museum related to the Wesleys is London's Museum of Methodism. There, in a small room in the museum, is Charles's organ—the one he used for many years to compose at least some of his thousands of hymns. Although this historical object is still in working order, I had to "listen" to the story it tells without actually being able to hear it played. But as I listened in silence, it told the story of hymnody and the importance of musical worship to the Christian experience.

Charles Wesley was born on December 18, 1707, one of nineteen children born to Susanna Wesley and her husband, Samuel. Charles was given a fine education and proved himself a standout student, first at Westminster School and then at Oxford's Christ Church college. Although he made little of his first year at Oxford, he experienced a spiritual awakening in his second year and cofounded what became known as the Holy Club, which soon counted both his brother John and a young George Whitefield among its members. The members of the club lived according to strict rules as they attempted to make the most of every moment, and they dedicated great amounts of time to Bible study and introspection. Because they followed prescribed and dedicated methods for promoting morality, they were referred to as "Methodists," a pejorative term they wore with pride. Although these young men were well intentioned in their efforts, they did not fully understand the truth that mere outward goodness cannot earn favor with God.[1] That would come later.

Charles was ordained in 1735 and traveled to the American colony of Georgia with

Statue of Charles Wesley in Bristol

his brother John. Although both were moral and upright men, neither had yet had a true conversion experience. To the contrary, both were fully trusting in their own efforts to please God rather than relying on the finished work of Christ. After being overcome by illness and depression, Charles returned to England after just six months in America, but he could not find spiritual peace. It was not for another three years, in 1738, that he began to grapple with the truth of justification by grace alone through faith alone, which he did under the encouragement of Moravian leader Peter Böhler. At one point Charles finally understood that he was not truly saved, and he put his faith in Christ Jesus and received salvation.[2] He responded to this fresh awareness of God's grace by writing a song, and though we do not know with certainty which one it was, many scholars believe it was that great hymn of wonder and praise "And Can It Be?"

And can it be that I should gain
An int'rest in the Savior's blood?
Died He for me, who caused His pain?
For me, who Him to death pursued?
Amazing love! how can it be
That Thou, my God, shouldst die for me?

Days later his brother John had a conversion experience of his own, and almost immediately the brothers began to preach the gospel of justification by grace alone through faith alone—a calling that would consume the rest of their lives. Much to the shock and chagrin of others, especially the clergy of the Church of England, they began to do this preaching outdoors, in town squares and open fields. Great crowds flocked to hear them, sometimes numbering in the thousands or even tens of thousands. Together with their friend George Whitefield and several colleagues, they sparked what became known as the Great Awakening, a revival that saw countless people become Christians in England and the New World— ground we have already covered in the chapter on Whitefield Rock.

From the beginning of his Christian life to his death, and even while he preached, Charles wrote hymns. Some of his best-known and well-remembered ones are "Hark! the Herald Angels Sing," "Christ the Lord Is Risen Today," "Jesus, Lover of My Soul," "Love Divine, All Loves Excelling," "Rejoice, the Lord Is King!" There are many, many others. Methodism became a movement marked not only by

gospel preaching but also gospel singing. The spiritual content was not just preached and read but was also sung. And Charles provided the Christian church with some of its best-known and best-loved songs.

The Museum of Methodism is housed in the crypt of Wesley's Chapel, next door to John's London home. It is directly across from the Bunhill Fields cemetery where many great Christian leaders are buried, so I first walked past the graves of John Owen, Thomas Goodwin, John Bunyan, and the Wesley brothers' mother, Susanna Wesley. I paused to read the amazing gospel presentation carved on the sides of Joseph Hart's grave marker. And then I crossed

Charles Wesley's organ

the road to the museum. Charles's organ can be found in a small side chapel. It's a compact instrument, around eight feet high and four feet across, with just fifteen pipes visible at the front. The keyboard remains out of sight behind a hinged door. Although the organ is still playable, a sign warns that it must not be played without permission. Lacking both the ability and the permission to play it, I left it in silence. As with so many of the objects I discovered in my travels, the organ itself is rather unremarkable—there are thousands of organs just like it, and many that are far grander and in far better condition. But as with all of the objects I spent time with, it had a story to tell me.

To hear what this organ had to tell me, I needed to picture Charles Wesley sitting behind the keyboard—something that was not difficult to do. He has a few lyrics and the beginning of a melody in his mind. He begins humming a few bars to himself, then plays them, joining lyrics with melody. Maybe this time it's "Ye servants of God, your Master proclaim, and publish abroad His wonderful name," or "O for a thousand tongues to sing My great Redeemer's praise." Over the course of his life, Charles repeated this pattern thousands and thousands

of times, many of them sitting before this little organ. It's a joy to consider that some of the songs we consider classics began just here and just like that.

Wesley is only one of the many hymn writers who have given us songs through which we express our praise to God. The good news of the gospel is so good that it's not enough to talk and write about it—we must also sing it, with conviction and passion. And because of men and women like Wesley and Watts and Gadsby and Crosby and so many others, we can sing in innumerable ways. Wesley's simple organ reminded me that when I stand to sing and worship today, I do not stand alone. Rather, I sing in unity with brothers and sisters from many nations, and with believers from across all the ages. If I listen I can hear a chorus that extends across the whole history of the church.

One of Wesley's dear friends was also a mentor to his wife and a generous benefactor to his work. A short drive to the city of Bath would take me to the place where I could see and remember the role she played in the history of Christianity, and where I could consider how God has so often used patrons and benefactors to advance his cause.

21

SELINA HASTINGS'S MEMORIAL TOKEN

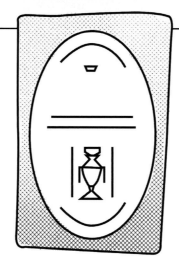

My journey around the world took me to many exhibits and museums. While some were utterly unique and especially fascinating, many of them were rather bland, and soon I found a lot of them blurring together in my memory. I had expected to visit some of the world's most famous and renowned museums, of course, and I planned to visit several smaller ones dedicated to noteworthy historical figures or movements. But what I hadn't expected to visit was a museum dedicated almost entirely to the architecture of a single city. I'll confess, I had no particular interest in the subject of the museum, but I did have interest in the building itself. Also, I was eager to see what I could find in one tiny, almost-forgotten room within the building.

The Museum of Bath Architecture has nothing to do with the architecture of restrooms or bathing facilities (though, frankly, that might have interested me more). Rather, it is a museum dedicated to the architecture of the city of Bath in Somerset, England. And the museum is housed in one of the many church buildings designed and funded by one of Christian history's great philanthropists, Selina Hastings, the Countess of Huntingdon. This museum is set in a residential neighborhood on a busy city street, and it houses some of the very few objects related to Hastings that have survived the years. Through these objects I heard a bit of her story, and through her story I began to better understand the crucial role philanthropy has played in the support and spread of Christian ministry through the ages.

Born as Selina Shirley on August 13, 1707, Selina was one of three daughters of the 2nd Earl Ferrers, and though her family was extremely wealthy, they were also extremely unhappy. Selina's mother left her father when Selina was just a young child. In 1728, at the age of twenty, Selina married Theophilus Hastings, the 9th Earl of Huntingdon, and unlike the marriage of her parents, her own marital union brought great happiness to her and her husband. They would have seven children together. As a couple, the Hastingses were engaged in the very highest strata of polite, wealthy British society.[1]

Although Selina was dutiful in carrying out the religious obligations expected of her, it was not until she was in her early thirties in 1739 that she experienced a crisis of faith that would lead to her conversion. Selina had an opportunity to hear the young George Whitefield preach, and then to hear her sister-in-law share her testimony of newfound faith in Christ. It was only after these two events that Selina realized she had not fully grasped the gospel and had been relying on her own goodness to secure her standing with God. Her subsequent conversion was absolute and profound.[2] Although she remained committed to the established Church of England, she also made many friends among the new movement of Methodists, especially the Wesley brothers and George Whitefield. Selina was at first a close follower of John Wesley but over time became concerned about his belief in Christian perfectionism and gravitated toward Whitefield. He would later become her personal chaplain.

Selina's husband, Theophilus, died in 1746, making her a widow at the age of just thirty-nine. Although she desperately loved her husband and grieved his death for the rest of her life, his death marked the beginning of a new mission for her, one that would consume the remainder of her days. Blessed with both a high social position and tremendous wealth, she committed herself to deploying each of these resources toward the causes that were closest to her heart: the evangelism of her aristocratic peers and the financial support of Christian ministry. In the years that remained to her, she used the vast majority of her income and her wealth to fund a host of Christian causes. She supported seminarians who were engaged in their studies; she was instrumental in founding and funding Wales's Trevecca College; she supported Methodist pastors and evangelists in their itinerant ministries; she worked to find, send, and finance foreign missionaries; she gave

The pulpit at Selina Hasting's Bath Chapel where George Whitefield delivered the inaugural sermon

© Stephen McCaskell

generously to those who were poor and in need; and she funded the building of chapels. Remarkably, she carried out all of these deeds while suffering chronic pain and terrible loss, outliving all but one of her dear children.

In this era, the preaching of great evangelists like Wesley and Whitefield was drawing great crowds to the Christian faith. Because not nearly enough buildings were available to house the crowds of people and the new congregations, Selina took it upon herself to fund, or at least to secure funding for, as many of them as she could. She sought out and hired pastors to preach and fill the pulpits, and by the end of her life she had 116 chapels built and filled as

Framed memorial token

part of her "Connexion." As many as sixty-four of the buildings were funded by her hard work and endless generosity.[3] Sadly, few of these still stand, and to my knowledge none remain as active churches today.

Her beloved Bath Chapel remains standing, though it has now been repurposed as the Museum of Bath Architecture. As I parked nearby and walked toward the museum, I saw that the beautiful gate outside bears the inscription "Countess of Huntingdon Chapel" and a small plaque on the building itself says, "Here lived Selina, Countess of Huntingdon." While these modest quarters were never her primary residence, she did use them often when visiting Bath. Inside, surrounded by exhibits displaying the history of Bath architecture from ancient times to today, is a towering pulpit, fixed where it was when George Whitefield climbed its steps to lead the inaugural service at the chapel on October 6, 1765. I was able to stand in the pulpit, and it was a thrill to survey the building from that vantage point. Three great stone eagles stand before it, engraved with the initials of three people who were especially dear to her: her father, her daughter, and her husband. An alcove nearby marks "Nicodemus' Corner," where a curtain once protected curious bishops who wanted to hear evangelical preaching while remaining hidden from the eyes of the congregation. And in the back, almost forgotten, standing between the exhibits and the restrooms, is a small room dedicated to Selina's memory, as the building's founder.

Inside this room you can find a beautiful clock that she presented to the chapel when it opened. Nearby there is a copy of a hymnbook, a shortened form of the larger work she commissioned for use in her chapels. And finally, in a frame, is a memorial token. This token perhaps best summarizes the generous life of this wealthy countess, for it is very unostentatious. Upon her death, mourners were given simple cards in her memory, and this memorial token is a silk variation of one of those plain paper ones. It states, "Her body is buried in Peace, But her Name liveth evermore." A verse from the great hymn writer Joseph Hart brings comfort:

Forbear, my friends, to weep,
Since death has lost its sting;
Those Christians that in Jesus sleep,
Our God will with him bring.

Perhaps the most noteworthy feature of the exhibit is how small it is and how few objects it contains. Even this small collection is probably more than Selina would have wanted. When she died in 1791 at the age of eighty-three, she was buried according to her wishes—no extravagant coffin, no grand funeral, and no great tombstone. Only three people witnessed her burial next to her husband.[4] The vast majority of her wealth had been exhausted. But what remained was her legacy of faithful philanthropy.

As I looked at the memorial token from her memorial services and thought of this woman and her great wealth, tirelessly expended for the spread of the gospel, I was reminded that much of Christian ministry depends on the generosity of God's people, and that where much has been given, much is required. The Countess of Huntingdon was one of many people throughout the centuries to whom the Lord has given not only the gift of great wealth but also the accompanying gift of generosity. And like so many others, she chose not to spend that wealth on her own comforts and priorities but committed it all to God's purposes with eagerness and joy. That little token told a great story and even reminded me of the generosity of the benefactors who had allowed me to undertake this journey—a journey that would next lead me north to an object that stirs both sorrow and joy, that shows humanity at its worst and its best.

22

BROOKES SLAVE SHIP MODEL

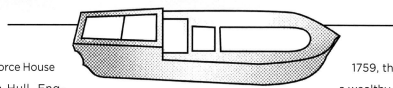

The Wilberforce House Museum in Hull, England, is dedicated to one great theme, the lifelong obsession of one great man. Housed in the birthplace and family home of William Wilberforce, it tells the horrific story of the transatlantic slave trade and one man's inexhaustible efforts to eradicate it. It houses many interesting historical objects that helped me get a feel for the day-to-day life of the man—a man I've studied extensively and who has challenged me in many ways. The museum includes a selection of Wilberforce's furniture, his personal library, and a number of his household goods. The museum also displays a series of artifacts that starkly tell of the barbarity of the slave trade: chains, shackles, and the manifests of ships whose cargo was men, women, and children. Among these Wilberforce household items and sober reminders of slavery is a small model ship, an object that would come to play a surprisingly prominent role in the abolition of the slave trade.

William Wilberforce was born on August 24, 1759, the eldest son of a wealthy merchant family. His father died while he was young, and with his mother unable to cope with the loss of her husband and the responsibility of raising a child, he was sent to live with an aunt and uncle in London. His aunt and uncle had quite recently come under the influence of the Methodist movement, and young William was intrigued by their religious convictions, eventually making his own profession of faith. Soon, however, William's mother became concerned about his growing religious enthusiasm and summoned him home. Before long he had abandoned his newfound faith and committed himself wholeheartedly to the pursuit of worldly pleasures.[1] He was educated at St. John's College, Cambridge, in preparation for a career in politics. By the age of twenty-one, he was serving as a member of the House of Commons, representing Hull. Three years later, he had been elected to represent the much bigger and more important riding of Yorkshire County.

Wilberforce was a classic extrovert. He loved to be surrounded by as many people as possible as often as possible. He was also a kind and interesting man who gathered friends and acquaintances and rarely missed an opportunity to meet new people. His friends loved to be in his presence and considered him the life of any party.[2] In his midtwenties he set out on an extended tour of Europe with his friend Isaac Milner. Milner was a committed Christian who simply acted and spoke freely about his Christian convictions while traveling in the presence of his companion. His words and example made Wilberforce reconsider and closely examine the claims of Christianity, and slowly he began to embrace the faith. By the closing months of 1785, Wilberforce was professing faith in Christ and exhibiting changed behavior, first in the use of his time and money.[3] He began to wonder if a career in politics could be reconciled with his new faith, and it was here that he made the wise decision to seek the counsel of John Newton.

Newton was a London pastor, a former slave trader who had been transformed by the grace of God and called to preach the gospel. His story is known, of course, from his great hymn "Amazing Grace." Newton assured Wilberforce that the Lord could and would use a committed Christian in politics.[4] His biographer tells how Wilberforce's faith provided him with a clear focus for the rest of his life: "His money, abilities, and power had been given to him by God, and he considered himself accountable in

the smallest detail for how he would now use them. His mission now was to apply Christian principles as he understood them to the world as he saw it around him."[5] By 1787 he had set himself two grand objectives: the reformation of "manners"—a way of referring to Christian morality at the time—and the abolition of the slave trade.

Wilberforce's campaign to see the slave trade abolished is a case study in showing patient endurance through trials and failure. It became an annual parliamentary tradition that he would bring forward a bill for abolition, which, for a variety of reasons, would fail year after year after year. But Wilberforce persisted, and a key part of his lifelong campaign was to expose the British public and the ruling elites of society to the true horrors of slavery. And this is where that model ship played an important role in our story.

Today, housed in a well-lit glass case on the second floor of the Wilberforce House Museum, a centerpiece of their collection, I found a model of a ship named the *Brookes*, a ship owned by the merchant Joseph Brooks and used to transport slaves. The *Brookes* took part in the "triangular route," where ships would sail from England to Africa carrying loads of manufactured goods. These goods would be exchanged for slaves who were then transported across the Atlantic to the Caribbean as a free and endless source of labor. Then, after the slaves had been off-loaded, the ships took aboard the raw materials produced in the colonies and returned to England, thus completing the triangle. The conditions for the slaves were horribly cruel, and vast numbers died en route. Many of those who survived the journey to the Americas were unfit to work.

Thomas Clarkson, a leading abolitionist and ally of Wilberforce, commissioned two models of the *Brookes* to visually display the conditions under which slaves were transported. One of these he kept for his own purposes and the other he gave to Wilberforce. It is this second model that is now on display at the museum.[6] The decks in the model have been cut away to show the cargo holds. And lying in those hold are miniature recreations of an incredible 454 people. The model shows the slaves squeezed together tightly on bare planks, with hands and feet shackled, in such a condition that they could not possibly move. The model highlights how these human beings were being treated in a manner worse than animals. Unbelievably, the *Brookes* would sometimes sail with an additional 150 people aboard in conditions that must have been beyond imagining and inconceivably horrifying.

Models and illustrations of the *Brookes* became one of the most powerful tools of abolition.[7] The model ship was a remarkable piece of propaganda, portraying the truth of the slave trade in a powerful way. It accomplished its purpose as Wilberforce and the other abolitionists insisted that people must look at the ship and

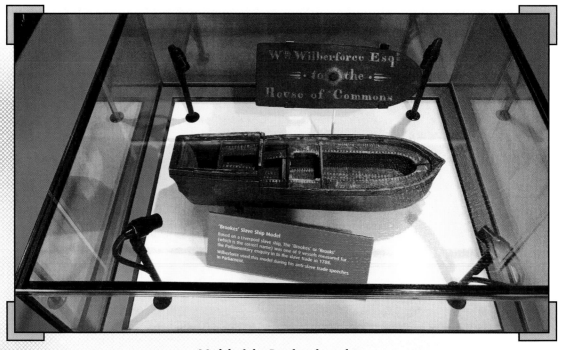

Model of the *Brookes* slave ship

visually acknowledge the reality of the African slave trade. They knew the truth would be shocking and believed that seeing the truth would demand action. And they were right. Although it took time and patience and careful strategizing, eventually the British public did come around to demand change. At long last both Parliament and the king were forced to respond. What had once seemed impossible became inevitable.

Wilberforce's Act for the Abolition of the Slave Trade finally succeeded on February 23, 1807, and it received royal assent a month later. Although it was a tremendous triumph for the man and his cause, it was incomplete, for it only stopped the trading of slaves by English ships while doing nothing for those who had already been sent overseas. It was not until 1833 that slavery itself was abolished and hundreds of thousands of slaves held in British colonies were finally set free. Fittingly, Wilberforce lived to hear that the passing of that final abolition bill had become certain. He received the news with joy and died peacefully three days later, a man who had committed his life to righting a great injustice and pursuing a great and worthy cause, a cause that was rooted in his convictions as a Christian.

Studying that model ship, I was not only reminded of the horrors of slavery, but I also remembered the story of this great man and his noble cause, a man with a passion to serve his fellow man and extend the respect and dignity those created in the image of God deserve, regardless of their skin color. Standing in Wilberforce House Museum, I could hear the story of Wilberforce and his life reverberating through that simple model ship. And beyond it, I could hear the story of how Christians have always been involved in pursuing justice and in addressing great evils. It is for good reason that I and others have drawn inspiration from the dogged determination and patient endurance of William Wilberforce.

And now it was time to consider how Christians have been concerned not only for their own people and nations but for people and nations far away. To tell that story I'd need to find objects both near and far, far away.

A QUICK LOOK:

LEMUEL HAYNES'S SERMON MANUSCRIPT

In my research for this project, I had a few restrictions. First, I wanted to focus on objects rather than locations, buildings, or memorials. And second, I wanted to focus on objects that are available to the general public.

Sometimes the lines blurred a bit. Some objects were not on display in a museum, but they *are* available on request. That was the case with a sermon manuscript held in the archives of the American Antiquarian Society in Worcester, Massachusetts.

Pastor Lemuel Haynes was an African American pastor of a white congregation. And in June 1805, while he was filling the pulpit of a nearby church, he was shocked to learn that a man named Hosea Ballou had been invited to lecture in his pulpit during his absence. This was upsetting because Ballou was a well-known proponent of universalism—the teaching that all of humanity will be saved regardless of what they do or believe. Haynes held to Calvinistic doctrine and would

later be known as "the Black Puritan" for his staunch theological orthodoxy. Upon learning of Ballou's visit, he hurried back to his church and arrived in time to hear Ballou deliver his heretical message. Invited to respond, Haynes stepped into the pulpit and delivered a satirical defense of orthodox doctrine. The sermon was titled "Universal Salvation, a Very Ancient Doctrine: With Some Account of the Life and Character of Its Author." The manuscript for the sermon, which was written in his own hand, is now in the holdings of the American Antiquarian Society.

After filling out the appropriate paperwork, the manuscript was removed from the archives and handed over for me to examine. For as long as I wanted, I could sit and read it. I studied it carefully, noting that it was written on tiny pieces of paper that were later stitched together. Despite the years, it remains in good condition. Although the paper shows some stains, it has not begun to crumble or decay.

It was a thrill to read this manuscript
of Lemeul Haynes's most famous sermon.

© Stephen McCaskell

Haynes's writing is bold and easy to decipher, and I had little trouble reading it.

His sermon in response to Ballou was preached to a small crowd in a small church, but it soon became a big deal. The manuscript was printed and distributed widely, and over the course of the next fifty years, it went through seventy editions.[1] I found it interesting that none of these later editions quite matched the text of the handwritten copy I was reading that day, indicating that this was likely the original copy and that Haynes had made some slight edits before declaring it fit to print. Because of that sermon and its many printings, Lemuel Haynes would become one of early America's foremost defenders of Christian doctrine.

23

ANDREW FULLER'S SNUFFBOX

The personal effects of some important historical figures have largely disappeared. John Calvin is one of history's towering figures, yet few objects remain that we can confidently link to him. Hudson Taylor changed the course of China, the world's most populated nation, but I was not able to track down as much as a single Bible he had once owned. There are other individuals, though, who have entire collections dedicated to their objects and accomplishments. William Carey is one of these.

I made the long journey to India, where Carey lived and died, to visit Serampore College and its museum. In that collection there are many objects from his life and ministry, but I mostly found myself closely examining Carey's desk and the letter box he used to organize his voluminous correspondence. Yet as exciting and interesting as those items were, it was on my journey through England that I found

an object that spoke particularly loudly. I stopped by the Angus Library of Regent's Park College in Oxford, which holds an outstanding collection of his artifacts. I lingered over a first edition of his Bengali Bible and over the broken fragment of a sign that hung over his shop while he was still a shoemaker. I read a number of his letters and journals and studied one of his Bibles, which he stored in a box crafted from his old workbench. I also visited Hackleton, where I found a church he once ministered at and the pulpit he once preached from. And further along, in Moulton, there was a first edition of his most important book and another collection of his notes and letters.

But one object eluded me. I told the archivist at the Angus Library in Oxford, "There is one object I'd love to see, but I'm pretty sure it's lost: Andrew Fuller's snuffbox." With a twinkle in her eye, she informed me she thought she knew where that snuffbox was. It wouldn't be easy to find, but if we were able to make the right connections, we could track it down. That was a challenge I couldn't refuse!

I left Oxford, heading north to Kettering, and along the way began making phone calls, pleading my case to gain permission to a small museum at Fuller Baptist Church. A few hours later I arrived at the church and was welcomed in with, "You've come to see a snuffbox!" The pastor led me upstairs to a small museum. There I saw several cases of artifacts and objects covered in protective blankets, and as he pulled them aside, there it was—a little snuffbox. Triumph!

But why the interest in a small snuffbox? Because of the story it tells—the story that bridges the little town of Kettering to the great big nation of India.

William Carey was born on August 17, 1761, and was raised in Paulerspury, a small village in central England where a plaque marks the spot where his cottage once stood. At the age of fourteen, he was apprenticed to a cobbler in a nearby village, and though Carey had been raised Anglican, he was persuaded by a fellow apprentice who was a Dissenter to leave the Church of England and join a Congregational church. This was the beginning of an important, lifelong spiritual pilgrimage.[1]

During Carey's time as an apprentice and shoemaker, he found that he was adept at languages and taught himself Greek, Hebrew, Italian, Dutch, and French. In 1783 he became

The signboard that once hung above William Carey's shop
© Stephen McCaskell

a Baptist, and by 1789 he was serving full-time as a pastor. After reading Jonathan Edwards's account of the life of David Brainerd, as well as the journals of the explorer James Cook, he became increasingly interested in foreign missions, and in 1792 he published his most enduring work, *An Enquiry into the Obligations of Christians to Use Means for the Conversion of the Heathens*.[2] This book outlined Christians' obligation to do missions, shared a brief history of mission work, gave statistical data about the world's need for such work, provided answers to objections against doing it, and contained a proposal for the kind of society that could be formed to support such an effort.[3]

Andrew Fuller's snuffbox

That same year, Carey preached a sermon with a particularly memorable phrase in it, a quote that has since become indelibly associated with his name: "Expect great things from God; attempt great things for God." In the fall of that same year, Carey formed the Baptist Missionary Society, and this is where that small snuffbox plays a fascinating role in the history of Christianity. Carey was not the only person in England who felt a deep burden for foreign missions. In October of 1792, he met with several other local pastors, including Andrew Fuller. Fuller took the minutes for the meeting, and I was able to read them from Fuller's journal in the Angus Library. Here's how he described that meeting.

> At a Ministers Meeting at Kettering the following resolutions were agreed to.
>
> 1. Desirous of making an effort for the propagation of the gospel among the heathen, agreeably to what is recommended in brother Carey's late publication on that subject, we, whose names appear to the subsequent subscription, do solemnly agree to act in society together for that purpose.
>
> 2. As in the present divided state of Christendom, it seems that each denomination, by exerting itself separately, is most likely to accomplish the great ends of a mission, it is agreed that this society be called The Particular Baptist Society for Propagating the Gospel among the Heathen.
>
> 3. As such an undertaking must needs be attended with expense, we agree immediately to open a subscription for the above purpose, and to recommend it to others.

A "subscription" was a means of funding the society, and as indicated they began collecting funds immediately. Those in attendance at the meeting had no collection basket on hand, so Fuller passed around his snuffbox instead. A snuffbox was simply a convenient way for an eighteenth-century gentleman to hold his snuff—a type of powdered tobacco that would be "snuffed" into the nose instead of smoked into the lungs. The box itself is ovular in shape, made of bone, and worn by age. Strangely, its lid has a depiction of the conversion of the apostle Paul. In this case the snuffbox is meaningful not for its original purpose but for the function it served on this October day in 1792. The men gathered that day put what they had in their pockets into the box, and it amounted to £13 2s. 6d. (approximately $2,500 today). It enabled the small beginning of what would become one of the largest and most important missionary movements in history.

Carey used these funds to sail to India the following April, never again to return to his native England. Over the next forty-one years, he accomplished a remarkable amount of work in India, training, teaching, and translating the Scripture. For good reason, he is considered the father of modern missions. His assistance with translation enabled the translation of the Bible into nearly all of India's major languages. He sought to end several inhumane practices throughout India, including infanticide and the burning of widows, and he founded Serampore College, which trained Indians in theology and liberal arts, and remains open today. However, as Mark Galli reminds us, his greatest impact would be felt in the generations that followed him: "His greatest legacy was in the worldwide missionary movement of the nineteenth century that he inspired. Missionaries like Adoniram Judson, Hudson Taylor, and David Livingstone, among thousands of others, were impressed not only by Carey's example, but by his words 'Expect great things; attempt great things.' The history of nineteenth-century Protestant missions is in many ways an extended commentary on the phrase."[4] Carey expected great things from God and on that basis attempted great things; thousands would follow his lead.

While Carey was not the first Protestant missionary, he served as a catalyst for a whole new movement. Generations of Christians were inspired by Carey's example and followed him from the safety and comfort of England and America to foreign lands. Over the next century, the missionary movement he sparked would reach almost every coastland on earth with countless souls being saved. It would make Christianity a truly global faith.

Remembering and honoring many of the men and women I encountered in my study for their accomplishments is a good thing. Yet Carey would not want me to put the accent on what he had done. His passion was to point others to Christ and give glory to God. Not long before he died, he scolded a friend: "You have been saying much about Dr. Carey and his work. When I am gone, say nothing about Dr. Carey; speak about Dr. Carey's Saviour." In a strange, strange way, that snuffbox did just that. It was a bizarre and unexpected object that in its own way marked the beginning of something far bigger than itself, something that would spread to the ends of the earth.

24

THE SLAVE BIBLE

Not all of the objects I saw on my travels had a positive story to tell. The Slave Bible is one of those. It's a story that warns us of the dangers of compromising the message of the gospel to accommodate our sin. And it's a timely reminder that sinful human beings can use good things—even the precious Word of God—to commit great evil.

Any fair reading of the Bible must conclude that one of its most prevalent themes is reconciliation. In fact, the great message of the gospel is that Jesus Christ has made a way for sinful humanity to be reconciled to a holy God. This great and ultimate reconciliation then allows and demands many other forms of reconciliation. In the pages of the New Testament, we read of Jews and gentiles, age-old enemies, worshiping together as brothers and sisters in the Lord. We read of Jewish apostles proclaiming a common faith with soldiers of the Roman army that had conquered them (Acts 10).

The reconciliation of the gospel is so great that Paul powerfully declared, "There is neither Jew nor Gentile, neither slave nor free, nor is there male and female, for you are all one in Christ Jesus" (Galatians 3:28). The great future promise of Christ's gospel is a day when God's people will gather before him as "a great multitude that no one could count, from every nation, tribe, people and language" (Revelation 7:9).

Sadly, those who proclaim Christ have often failed to admit, embrace, or pursue this kind of reconciliation. In fact, many Christians have oppressed other human beings—even other professing Christians—and they have co-opted the Bible to support their evil. A stunning example of this is on display at the Museum of the Bible in Washington, DC. The museum opened in 2017, and while there are thousands of items on display, the museum curators soon noticed one exhibit in particular that was generating an extraordinary amount of attention, so they moved the object out of the general collection and into a special exhibit. What was the object? It's the Slave Bible of 1808, part of the collection of Fisk University, but at the time I visited, on display at the Museum of the Bible.[1]

We have read about the unflagging efforts of abolitionists like William Wilberforce working to end the importation of slaves to the British colonies. And we learned that the Act for the Abolition of the Slave Trade succeeded on February 23, 1807. However, while this Act ended the slave trade, it did not free those who were already enslaved—generations of African people who had been forcibly removed from their homes and sold into a horrid, inescapable life of slavery. As slavery continued in British-held territories, some people expressed concern for the souls of these slaves. As was the custom of the day, they formed societies to reach them, and among them was the Society for the Conversion of Negro Slaves, a group that aimed to convert and educate slaves who had been transported to the Caribbean. As missionaries worked among the slaves of the British-owned islands, such as Jamaica and Barbados, they naturally wanted to introduce people to the Bible. Yet this introduced a problem. How could these missionaries teach the Bible to slaves without condemning slavery and therefore angering the slave owners? How could they show concern for souls while hiding what the Bible taught about slavery from the slaves themselves? How could they share the gospel while upholding the economic interests of their empire?

In 1807 the London publisher Law and Gilbert provided the answer with the first printing of *Parts of the Holy Bible, Selected for the Use of the Negro Slaves, in the British West-India Islands*, which had been commissioned by the Society for the Conversion of Negro Slaves. Today we know this simply as the "Slave Bible."[2] The official title of this edition optimistically declares that it shares "parts of the Holy Bible," but it would be more accurate to say that it *removes* parts. This was a "Bible" radically truncated to remove any passages or verses that condemned slavery or condoned racial equality. So pervasive is the message of freedom in the Word of God that only 232 of the Bible's 1,189 chapters made the final cut. Gone was the story of Israel's exodus from captivity in Egypt; gone were prohibitions against stealing and selling human beings; gone were passages demanding fair wages and freedom during years of Jubilee. Also gone were passages emphasizing reconciliation between all humanity as a duty and privilege of the Christian faith. And, of course, gone was the beautiful throne room vision of all humanity, every skin color and ethnic group, assembled before God. What remained in the Slave Bible? Biblical descriptions of servitude and slavery, of course. Absent the portions that had been removed, these could be used as divinely inspired proof that God endorses slavery. Or, at the very least, the Slave Bible could be used to give the slaves the message of reconciliation with God without the accompanying message of reconciliation with man.

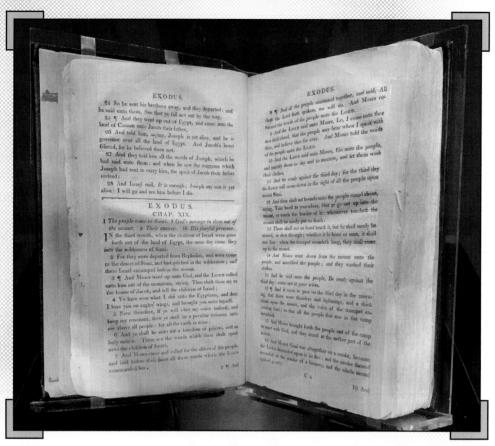

The Slave Bible

It could give them enough to save their souls but not enough to free their bodies.

This seemed like the best of both worlds for those eager to carry out the work of missions to slaves. They could share "the Bible" with those enslaved while still protecting the system of slavery. Slaves could grasp the broad outline of the Bible, but they were not given those parts that might prove disruptive or that might incite rebellion. The Slave Bible allowed white missionaries to show concern for souls even while their masters still enslaved their bodies. As such, the Slave Bible was not truly the Word of God, for it protected an exploitive system by committing the evil act of tampering with God's Word. Conspicuously absent from the Slave Bible is Revelation 22 and its grave prohibition against adding to or subtracting from God's Word.

At the time I visited the Museum of the Bible, the Slave Bible had been given its own exhibit. It was the lone object on display, surrounded by placards that share its story and significance. The book sits in a glass case, propped open, and as I studied the words on the open pages, I immediately understood why the curators had left it open to this particular spot, for it made a jarring point. At the top of the left page are the closing verses of Genesis 45, where Jacob, now aware that Joseph is alive, determines that he will go to Egypt to find him. But Genesis 45 gives way to Exodus 19, which describes the Israelites approaching Mount Sinai, having already left Egypt. What's missing? The entire account of the Israelite captivity in Egypt, their brutal mistreatment as an enslaved people, God's punishment upon Pharaoh and his nation, and the miraculous delivery of God's people in crossing the Red Sea.

I was visiting the museum at opening time, so the large crowds that are often there had not yet gathered. I stood for some time in the dimly lit room, alone but for a single museum employee, and pondered the strange contrast this book represents. While passages of the book are taken from the Bible, which is inspired by God, at the same time, this is not the Bible. It is an intentional and manipulative reduction of God's truth, a Bible that has been brutally truncated to present a false gospel message. By stripping the Bible of so many of its words, the Bible has been stripped of its power. It teaches a truncated gospel—one that promises reconciliation with God but without the demand of reconciliation with man, much less an affirmation of universal human worth and value as people made in the image of God. Far from an object to celebrate, it's a sober reminder of the lengths human beings will go to hide and cover their sin. And while it's a simple artifact, it tells a story much larger than itself. It told me of the evils of slavery and the long legacy of this horrific practice within "Christian" nations. Knowing that this great evil was often perpetuated by those who called themselves after the name of Christ humbled me. Likewise, considering that many of those who disagreed with slavery remained silent rather than risk their reputation by speaking up humbled me. And the Slave Bible reminded me that Christians must teach and know and proclaim the whole counsel of God in every generation. Moreover, it warned me that I, too, may face the temptation to use the perfect revelation of God to pursue even the most imperfect, unjust ends.

A QUICK LOOK:

JOSIAH HENSON

As I spent months traveling around the world searching for historic objects that would tell me the story of Christianity, I began to wonder if there were any objects close to my home in Ontario, Canada. I knew that Christianity came to the land we know as Canada relatively late in the story, but I felt there had to be something here that was worth pursuing. A fortuitous coincidence led me to learn of a local man who had a significant role in Christian history, yet had somehow remained unknown to me, even though I have lived out my entire life in this area of Canada.

I learned of Josiah Henson from the author of a new biography written about him, who kindly sent me a copy to review.[1] Josiah Henson lived much of his life in Southern Ontario as a religious and civic leader among African Americans who had followed the Underground Railroad from slavery in America to freedom in Canada. Born in the United States, Henson lived most of his life in Canada, and to this day he remains best known in the country of his birth under a different name: Uncle Tom.

Henson was born in Maryland in or around 1789.[2] From his first breath, he was the property of others, an object to be bought and sold, used and abused. And sadly, he was. When Henson was nine, he was torn from his mother and sold (though, thankfully, reunited with her before long).[3] As a young man, he was beaten so severely that he was permanently maimed. But he endured. As he grew in age and competence, he was given increasing trust and responsibility by the man who owned him. Yet his owner soon fell on hard times and transferred his slaves to his brother's farm in Kentucky. The brother attempted to sell Henson to a plantation in New Orleans, and he was saved from this fate only through the timely sickness of his master's son.[4]

Henson knew that his life was at the mercy of his owners, and he realized that he needed to make a break for his freedom. With his wife and four children, he made the long, terrifying journey to Canada, eventually crossing the Niagara River in 1830. Free at last and determined to make the most of this newfound freedom, he helped to found a settlement for freedmen in

Dawn Township, Upper Canada. This community became home to the British-American Institute, which educated former slaves and their children and trained them in useful trades. Henson served as one of the leaders of the institution and the community while overseeing several farms, mills, and other industries. He became an important leader among blacks and escaped slaves in Canada and beyond.[5]

And that was just the beginning. Converted to Christianity as a teenager, Henson became a Methodist preacher and traveled far and wide to preach to whites and blacks alike. He made several journeys into the American South to help rescue other slaves. He traveled to England for business and ministry, dined with the archbishop of Canterbury, had an audience with Queen Victoria, won a medal at the World Fair, and preached in Charles Spurgeon's pulpit.[6] In the midst of doing all these things, he also wrote an autobiography to share the story of his life. And that autobiography fell into the hands of a woman named Harriet Beecher Stowe. Stowe saw in Henson the seeds of a character for a new novel she was writing, and she named that character Uncle Tom. Stowe would go on to become, according to Abraham Lincoln, the little lady whose book would begin a great and terrible war—the American Civil War. Stowe's book stirred strong emotions against slavery leading to war and the eventual freeing of black slaves. And behind that war, that woman, and her key character, Uncle Tom, was the incredible life of Josiah Henson.

Portrait of Josiah Henson sitting next to an unidentified man, ca. 1876
Library of Congress, LOT 14022, no. 325

Today the Ontario Heritage Trust maintains Uncle Tom's Cabin Historic Site just outside the small town of Dresden. The cabin lies on the site of the settlement he founded and marks the place he lived and ministered for many years. In the midst of my travels around the world, I was amazed to find this marker of a key moment in Christian history just a few hours from my home. As I walked around the heritage site, exploring the buildings and learning about Henson at the Josiah Henson Interpretive Centre, I was moved and stirred by the life of this brave brother in Christ. The museum holds a small number of his effects, including a rare first edition of his autobiography and a signed portrait of Queen Victoria, her gift to him during his private audience with her at Windsor Castle. The queen told Henson she was familiar with his story (as, indeed, her diaries record), and she was especially fascinated with his long endurance and many accomplishments despite such terrible suffering. For his part, Henson considered her "the living symbol of emancipation and freedom," a just ruler who led the nation in which he had been welcomed.[7]

I left the historic site feeling an appropriate measure of pride in my country, Canada, for the role it played welcoming slaves at the end of the Underground Railroad. Canada was a place of shelter and freedom for many former slaves, giving them a new chance at life. I was especially moved by Henson's description of his reaction upon crossing the border near Niagara: "I threw myself on the ground, rolled in the sand, seized handfuls of it and kissed them, and danced around, till, in the eyes of several who were present, I passed for a madman."[8] But Henson's joy was not that of a madman; it was the unspeakable joy of a free man. And who can blame him for celebrating what was now his?

25

DAVID LIVINGSTONE'S WRITING BOX

There are two museums in the world today that have substantial exhibits dedicated to David Livingstone. One is in Scotland, where Livingstone was born and spent his youth and early adult years, and the other is in Livingstone, Zambia, on the African continent he is famous for exploring. I had every intention of visiting both locations until I learned that the David Livingstone Centre at Blantyre, Scotland, had been closed for refurbishment and would remain that way for a number of years. So I focused my attention on the museum in Zambia and packed my bags for Africa. The journey from my home in Canada was long but very rewarding.

The Livingstone Museum is situated in the town now named after the British explorer and missionary, just minutes from the border with Zimbabwe and the mighty Victoria Falls. The museum contains several galleries related to history, archaeology, ethnography, and the natural world. But best of all, at least to my interests, was the gallery dedicated to David Livingstone. It contains a number of his personal effects, including a cloak and hat he wore while exploring, the surgical kit he always carried with him, and a selection of the letters he wrote. Like many places I visited, I spent time examining different objects, learning about their history, and listening for a story that would help me better understand this man and his moment in Christian history. What captured my attention, and what I believe powerfully tells the tale of his life and influence, is his traveling box.

To our twenty-first-century minds, it is almost impossible to imagine a time when world maps had vast areas marked with the words *terra incognita*—unknown land. This was a time before aircraft and satellites, and unmapped, uncharted territory had to be explored on foot, often at great expense and at great peril.

Tin traveling box of David Livingstone

Explorers were regarded as dashing, heroic figures who disappeared for months or years at a time, then reemerged with fantastical tales of what they had seen and experienced. Some of these explorers did their work for the sake of fame, but others did it for the sake of a higher cause, often their desire to share their faith. The best known of these missionary explorers is David Livingstone.

Livingstone was born in Blantyre, Scotland, in 1813, the son of poor but godly parents. By the age of ten, he was helping to provide for his family, doing dangerous work at a cotton factory. An ambitious boy, he engaged his studies each night and progressed well in his education,

developing a particular interest in the study of the natural world. He professed faith in Christ at a young age and soon felt a special call: "In the glow of love that Christianity inspires, I resolved to devote my life to the alleviation of human misery."[1] This misery would be addressed by the three related themes that would soon come to dominate his life: evangelization, exploration, and emancipation.[2]

Determined to serve God in medical missions, Livingstone trained as a doctor, was ordained as a missionary, and was sent to southern Africa, arriving there in March 1841. He soon embarked on several missionary journeys and witnessed firsthand the terrible evidence of the slave trade, even deep in the African interior. Seeing the suffering of slavery was heartbreaking to him, and he resolved to do what he could to stop it. He believed there were two keys to destroying the African slave trade: the power of Christianity and the expansion of commerce in Africa. Christianity could change the hearts of the African people so they would consider slavery immoral, and the growth of commerce in Africa would provide people with material resources and financial opportunities more lucrative than selling fellow Africans to European slavers.[3]

Livingstone believed that developing and expanding African commerce depended on discovering navigable rivers that would extend deep into the continent and provide routes to deliver the riches of Africa to the markets of the world. He set out to explore these rivers, especially the mighty Zambezi, which flows through modern-day Angola, Zambia, Namibia, Botswana, Zimbabwe, and Mozambique. Two of his great journeys, which together consumed ten years of his life, were focused on the Zambezi. His first journey led him from Linyanti in central Africa to Luanda on the west coast, then across the width of Africa to Quelimane on the east coast, making him the first person in recorded history to cross the continent. He returned to England in 1856, now famous, and published a record of his journey titled *Missionary Travels and Researches in South Africa*. It became an immediate bestseller, and its popularity led to tremendous public influence.

While in Zambia, we crossed the bridge to Zimbabwe to see the statue of David Livingstone at the top of Victoria Falls.

Livingstone began his second expedition along the Zambezi in 1858, and though it did not accomplish all he had hoped, it furthered his fame when he returned and published his next work, *Narrative of an Expedition to the Zambesi and Its Tributaries*. His third and final great expedition was meant to discover the source of the Nile. The journey lasted from 1866 to 1873, when Livingstone finally succumbed to illness in what is today northern Zambia. His body was returned to England, where he was given the honor of a hero's burial in Westminster Abbey.

If you happen to visit Livingstone, Zambia, and have the appropriate visa, you can walk across the bridge to Victoria Falls, Zimbabwe. While there, visit Victoria Falls National Park, and you'll find a large statue of Livingstone. Back in Zambia, you'll find another statue of him near the top of the Zambian falls. Which side of the falls offers the better views? Most seem to say Zimbabwe, but it depends on the time of the year, the flow of the water, and the amount of spray in the air.

The Livingstone Museum, located in the city still named in his honor, houses a little box that played an important role in his writing, and in that way, in his expanding, worldwide fame and the influence it afforded him. I stood before it for a long time and studied it to hear what it would tell me about the man and his role in Christian history. Livingstone's traveling box is a simple and unadorned tin box battered by wear and blackened by age. It played a crucial role in Livingstone's life, for it held his journal and served as his mobile desk on his long and perilous journeys. Whenever he stopped for the night, he would open the box, remove his journal, his pen, and a candle. Then he would close the lid and spread the journal on top of it. He'd set the candle on the corner of the box and light it. Looking closely at the box, I could see a small pile of wax that remains where the candle provided a light, undoubtedly dim but sufficient for his journaling. Livingstone would write his thoughts in journals and then later publish these, making fascinating reading for rich and poor alike. A tremendously gifted writer, he vividly described the many beauties and wonders of Africa—along with the innumerable horrors of slavery. Most English people could not travel to Africa themselves, but they eagerly made the journey vicariously through Livingstone's books.[4] As they read, he persuaded them of the evils of slavery and the humanity of the African people. He convinced them that Africa, far from a barbaric land, was able to advance into the modern world.[5] Through a traveling box, a journal, and a candle, he changed the way the English nation viewed the continent and its people. As I listened, this little box told a great story!

While I was in Zambia I met with a local pastor named Conrad Mbewe and asked him how today's Zambians regard Livingstone. After all, there is a long history of colonialism between European nations and today's African countries, and many people today are critical of the past. Mbewe's answer was helpful and fascinating. He pointed out that when Zambia became independent in 1964, most of the cities that had received British names during the days of the British Empire were given new African names—a rejection of British power and influence. But the town of Livingstone was a rare exception. Today, more than fifty years after Zambian independence, there is still no movement to change that. David Livingstone remains an honored figure in the lands to which he gave so much of his life, a lasting testimony to his love for the people of Africa and the work he did to change European attitudes toward Africa and its people.

From Africa my road would lead me back to India to a very different kind of missionary who aptly represents the countless thousands of women who have heeded the summons to take the gospel far from home and family to distant lands.

26

AMY CARMICHAEL'S PLAQUES

I know

Fear not

Ask Him.

A VERY PRESENT HELP.

Good and Acceptable

Of all the historical characters I encountered in my round-the-world journey, none of them blessed me more at a personal level than Amy Carmichael. I first crossed the Atlantic to visit her birthplace in a small seaside village in Northern Ireland, then followed her own journey to a church she helped found in Belfast. A visit to the Public Records Office of Northern Ireland led me to her precious Bible, covered in notes and highlights, and for an hour I sat, turning its pages, deeply moved to see and read the book that had sustained her through her most difficult times. But I wasn't finished there. I knew that I needed to see the work to which she had dedicated her life, so I packed for India—the land where she poured out her life for the sake of the gospel.

Amy Carmichael was born in 1867 in Millisle, Northern Ireland. A precocious and mischievous child, she enjoyed a privileged upbringing in a distinctly Christian home. She committed her life to Christ at boarding school while a teen, then returned home when her family fell on hard times.[1] In Belfast she became involved in ministering to the poor and in founding Welcome Evangelical Church, which remains open and active to this day. The family moved to Manchester where she again committed herself to serving the poor, but she soon grew in her conviction that God was calling her to serve as a foreign missionary.

In 1895 the Church of England Zenana Missionary Society welcomed Carmichael to India, and she remained in that land for the rest of her life. There she joined a missionary in his itinerant ministry and became responsible for discipling the female converts.[2] In her travels in India, she learned, to her horror, of young girls who were forced into ritual prostitution in Hindu temples. Carmichael took it as her personal mission to rescue these girls and to raise them in a safe environment as their *Amma*, or mother. She began this work in the city of Tirunelveli, and in 1927 founded Dohnavur Fellowship as an orphanage for girls, though it would soon expand to become a bustling center of all kinds of ministries.

I arrived in the southern Indian city of Thiruvananthapuram and was greeted outside the airport by two Christian friends of a friend who had offered to accompany me. One was a professional driver, both able and eager to navigate the tricky Indian road system, and the other was a kind believer willing to give a couple of days to showing me how God had worked in his part of the world. We had many hours of driving ahead of us, first to reach the extreme southern tip of India where we could rest for the night, then to locate Dohnavur Fellowship.

The next morning I was greeted at the front gates of the ministry by a man named Ezekiel, who would serve as my guide on the visit. I had imagined Dohnavur Fellowship as a compact campus with a few buildings, and was surprised to see buildings separated from one another with great open expanses between them. The Fellowship remains an active ministry center, serving as a church, an orphanage, and a bustling hospital. We soon met a woman named Me-Malar who told us her story. In 1948 she was brought to Dohnavur Fellowship and carried to Amy Carmichael, who held her in her arms, prayed for her, and gave her the name Me-Malar, which is Tamil for "beautiful

This is the bird bath that marks
Amy Carmichael's grave.

flower." Me-Malar grew up, dedicated her life to the ministry, and serves there still. She and Ezekiel showed us around and took us to visit Carmichael's grave. Although she wished to be buried in an unmarked plot, those who loved Amy Carmichael and knew of her love of birds had placed a simple birdbath on the grave to mark the spot. It was an appropriate marker.

Next they took us to the church, where Me-Malar played hymns for us on the bells high up in the steeple. We visited the hospital, where thousands of people continue to receive care every year. Best of all, they took us to Carmichael's living quarters, which have been preserved much as they were upon her death.

After a devastating fall in 1931, she was confined almost entirely to this room for the last twenty years of her life, and it was from this small space that she directed her ministry. Here she wrote her books and engaged in voluminous correspondence with people all over the world. Most importantly, it was here that she met with the myriad children who were brought to her for safekeeping.

Ezekiel showed me a scuffed area on the tiled floor that marked the spot where her bed had once rested, though the bed itself was in a nearby alcove and had been moved to make way for chairs and a table when the quarters serve as a meeting room. Above and all around the spot the bed had been, I couldn't help but notice pictures and Scripture passages, unmoved since Amy's death, each one significant to her in its own way. I recognized several of them from a book I had read, the first biography written in her honor.

One of the pictures was a painting of Switzerland's Matterhorn. This simple painting was a source of great encouragement and

Amy Carmichael's plaques

inspiration to her. She once wrote friends to say, "When I am in pain or too tired to find words, I look at a picture of the Matterhorn and the lake at its foot, and I let it pray for me for you. Let the strength of the mountains be theirs, the purity of the snows, the beauty of the blue water, the steadfastness of the rocks, the loveliness of the flowers on the banks and, above all, the joy of the little stream that flows forth to bless others."[3]

Nearby the painting were two plaques, one above the other, each with a pair of words painted on them: "I know" and "Fear not." Her friend Dr. Nancy Robbins had once heard Carmichael voice the fear that her injury had left her too great a burden, and that because of her infirmity she was impeding the work of the ministry. Her friend encouraged her with the words of Revelation 2, which include those phrases, "I know. . . . Fear not" (vv. 9–10 ASV). Carmichael had these words made into plaques and mounted above her bed. Later she wrote a poem about them.

> "I know": the words contain
> Unfathomable comfort for our pain.
> How they can hold such depths I do
>   not know—
> I only know that it is so.
> "Fear not": the words have power
> To give the thing they name; for in an hour
> Of utter weariness, the soul, aware of One
>   beside her bed,
> Is comforted.

> O Lord most dear,
> I thank Thee, and I worship—
> Thou art here.[4]

Of all that I had seen about her life and ministry, these two plaques seemed to best encapsulate them, to tell their story. They spoke of her great confidence that she was known by God, something far more than a knowledge of the facts of her life and existence, but a heartfelt knowledge of her struggles and circumstances. This was a source of great comfort for her as she suffered physical pain and as she found herself unable to do so much of what she loved to do.

Me-Malar was one of the final orphans Amy Carmichael personally welcomed to Dohnavur Fellowship.

And because God knew her, she had nothing to fear. Carmichael knew she need never be afraid, because her God was always with her, always present in her dark valleys. She was known and loved by God, so she could extend the knowledge of God and the love of God to others. And she did, faithfully, to her final days.

Amy Carmichael is just one among a host of Christian women, many whose names will not be remembered in history books, who have committed their lives to foreign missions. All through the history of Christianity, women have served not only as faithful partners and helpers to their husbands but as zealous workers for the gospel in their own right. I could not know or understand the story of Christian missions or, indeed, the Christian church, without accounting for the many women who have heard and heeded the call to go and make disciples. Amy Carmichael is a wonderful reminder of this crucial aspect of the Christian story.

India is just one of the world's great nations, and even as missionaries poured onto its shores to share the gospel, many also went to China. In China, one man's efforts to preach the good news about Jesus would transform not only the spiritual condition of that country, but forever alter the history of Christian missions. I knew I needed to travel there, as well, to continue the story that was unfolding before me.

A QUICK LOOK:

SPURGEON'S PREACHING RAIL

The Great Reformation sparked a renewed passion for preaching, and from that time until today (and, I hope, until the end of time), many of Christianity's great figures have also been her great preachers. But perhaps none of them has ever been the equal of Charles Spurgeon, who, for good reason, is considered the "prince of preachers." Although he lived for just fifty-seven years, he spent almost all of them preaching and, for the majority of his life, was Christianity's foremost personality. His devotionals, commentaries, and sermons are loved and appreciated to this day.

In the years since Spurgeon's death, his library and possessions have been scattered far and wide. I encountered several of them in London where Spurgeon lived and died, but found some even as far away as South Africa. It might surprise some to learn that the most substantial collection of Spurgeon artifacts is located in Kansas City, Missouri, in the Spurgeon Library of Midwestern Baptist Theological Seminary.

I visited in a season when it was cold and snowy at home but beautiful and sunny (though still not insufferably hot) in Kansas City. I was welcomed into the newly built Spurgeon Library, which was constructed specifically to hold a substantial part of Spurgeon's own collection. Several volumes lie open in display cases, including a few in which he had jotted witty but scathing remarks. For example, he had crossed out the subtitle of one commentary ("Designed as a help to a better understanding of the sacred writings") and provided his own: "Adapted to blind the eye and prevent the truth in Jesus from shining upon the soul." He also crossed out the author's academic credentials and substituted "Arminian Twister of the Word." In a display just outside the door is a personal copy of *The Pilgrim's Progress*, which he claimed to have read at least a hundred times. This one is pocket-sized and is clearly bent as if it spent much of its time within Spurgeon's coat pocket.

The largest and most prominently displayed

object in the library is a preaching rail that was taken from Waterbeach Chapel many years before. It was there, on the outskirts of Cambridge, that Spurgeon took up his first pastorate while still only sixteen years old. It is a thin rail, almost like a bannister, supported by seven decorative columns, and is perfectly symmetrical. In the center it supports a pair of platforms, one flat and one angled, that together make up the pulpit. And it was from right here that Spurgeon first preached as a pastor. It was from here that he began the ministry that would define him but, far more importantly, reach so many minds and hearts. From his earliest days, when he was so young that today he wouldn't yet be able to drive himself to church, he was committed to preaching the Word of God. Although he had many other passions and carried out many other ministries, all of them would be supplemental to his preaching. This rail aptly shows his unwavering commitment to that great and noble task.

Spurgeon's preaching rail at the Spurgeon Library of
Midwestern Baptist Theological Seminary

27

HUDSON TAYLOR'S GRAVE

The speedometer of the bullet train stood at 300 kilometers per hour as I was whisked across the Chinese countryside from Shanghai to Zhenjiang. The skies were dark and gloomy above the cities, towns, and villages that briefly appeared for a moment and then were gone again as I looked through the windows of our speeding train. Arriving, I stood on the platform of the station 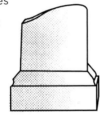 in Zhenjiang and, looking out across the city, saw a great tower with a cross on top of it rising above the nearby homes and businesses. Opening my umbrella in the falling rain, I began walking toward Xuande Church to visit the stirring memorial to the great missionary Hudson Taylor.

Although Taylor was not the first missionary to China, there is little doubt he was the most prominent and influential. The organization he founded and the missionary methods he established drove missionary activity in China for decades after his death. Through his work and influence, countless Chinese people came to Christ, and in the tower in Xuande Church and the exhibit it contains, I saw both the success of Hudson Taylor and the complexity of Chinese Christianity. It's a story of the gospel going east and a reminder of the ongoing shifts we are seeing in Christianity today.

Hudson Taylor was born in the Yorkshire town of Barnsley, England, on May 21, 1832, the oldest of four siblings. His father, James, was a chemist by trade, though he was also a Wesleyan minister who traveled most weekends to preach at nearby churches. His mother, Amelia, was a kind and gentle soul who loved her children and was wholly committed to their physical and spiritual welfare. Although Taylor would not learn this fact until he was older, his parents had consecrated him to the Lord before he was born, and particularly to mission work in

The Hudson Taylor Tower

rose from his knees a changed man and soon afterward sensed God calling him to ministry in China. "Never shall I forget the feeling that came over me then. Words could not describe it. I felt I was in the presence of God, entering into a covenant with the Almighty. . . . And from that time the conviction has never left me that I was called to China."[2] After several years of preparation and a long sea voyage, Taylor arrived in Shanghai on March 1, 1854.

Taylor would serve the people of China until his death in 1905. His analysis of the weaknesses of missionary strategies there would lead him to reject the methods of his fellow Western missionaries and found the China Inland Mission, which would become the region's foremost missionary organization. (Today China Inland Mission continues its work as OMF International.) He would make the radical and controversial decision to leave behind his English clothing and customs and instead adopt the dress, style, and customs of the Chinese. It was an unusual strategy for that time, but one that proved effective, even as it aroused the mockery of many of his peers.[3] In addition, Taylor refused to solicit funds or engage in campaigns to secure donations, preferring to remain entirely dependent on God's provision. He embraced missionaries who shared his convictions from across denominational lines. Through it all, he began to see a great movement among the Chinese people toward Christianity, then a crushing rebellion meant to stamp it out. He married twice in his life, burying one wife and several children in

China. "Dear God," they prayed, "if you should give us a son, grant that he may work for you in China."[1]

At first an answer to this prayer seemed doubtful. As a young man, Taylor took a job as a bank clerk and quickly found himself drawn to religious skepticism and worldly materialism. He began to turn away from the faith of his parents, but those who loved him, his mother and sister in particular, prayed earnestly for him. One day young Hudson came upon a tract and was gripped by the simple words written on it, "It is finished." As he read he understood that Christ's redeeming work was done and that there was nothing for him to do but fall to his knees and turn to Christ in repentance and faith. Taylor

China. He himself died and was buried next to his first wife, Maria, and four of their children in a small cemetery. Years passed and eventually the cemetery was abandoned, covered over by warehouses, and forgotten.

But then something unexpected happened. In the 1980s, Taylor's descendants toured China and found his gravestone in the Zhenjiang museum. In 2012 a Chinese businessman got in touch with them to tell them he had found and purchased Maria's gravestone at a local antique shop. Then, in 2013, with the conditions of the warehouses deteriorating, the buildings were torn down and the Taylor family was given permission to excavate the land. Very soon they uncovered the bodies of Hudson and Maria, whose remains were moved to nearby Xuande Church, where a Hudson Taylor Memorial Tower was built to serve as their final resting place.[4] The tower opened in 2018, and today it stands as a powerful tribute to a man whose life profoundly influenced the history of missions and the growth of Christianity in China.

Xuande Church is today associated with the Three-Self Patriotic Movement, the government-sanctioned church in China. Such churches agree to abide by a number of government regulations, including government surveillance and adherence to the principles of socialism. Yet this is a church that has decided to celebrate Taylor's life and influence, and the church has several objects and artifacts that remember the man and his ministry. I explored the tower and found that it contains beautiful and stirring

Graves of Hudson and Maria Taylor

exhibits describing the long and difficult labor of the early missionaries. One section deliberately, powerfully shows how the success of those early missionaries depended wholly on specific answers to specific prayers. But at the center of it all are the graves of Hudson and Maria, with their recovered gravestones rising above them. Hudson's is still whole and intact, while Maria's is broken and faded. But they are now there, side by side in death, even as they were united in ministry in life.

Not long after Taylor died, China became a Communist nation and there was a wholesale rejection of Christianity. Foreign missionaries were driven out and believers forced to worship in secret, yet the church continued to grow, going "underground" in hiding from the governmental authorities. Even repeated outbreaks of harsh persecution could not stamp out what Taylor and so many other faithful Christians had begun. And while I'm thankful I could visit this tower and pay tribute to such a godly man, I expect that he, like many we've encountered in our journey, would be untroubled by the fact that his grave was forgotten for so long and his body lost. Hudson Taylor had little concern for the remains of his body or his own legacy. His passion was for the eternal souls of the people of China and the glory of God. Fittingly, the wall behind his grave is marked by his own words, an expression of that passion: "If I had a thousand pounds China should have it; if I had a thousand lives China should have them; No! not China, but Christ. Can we do too much for Him? Can we do enough for such a precious Saviour?" His life and his death answered the questions.

The next stop on my long journey would be in faraway California so I could consider the start of a very different movement and one that rapidly expanded across the entire globe.

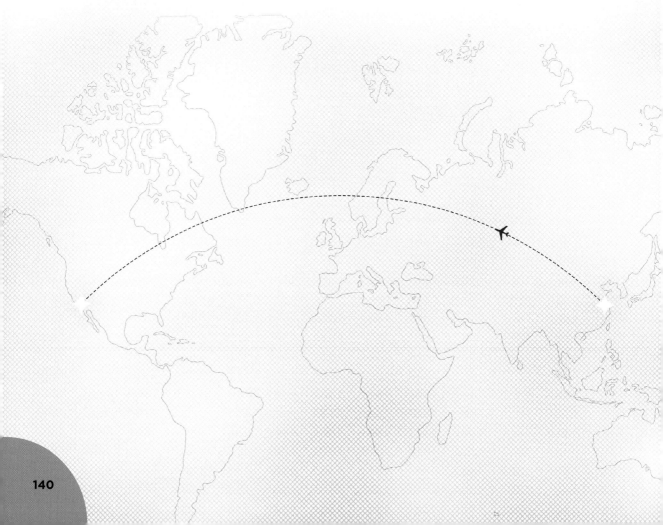

A QUICK LOOK:
GEORGE MÜLLER'S COLLECTION BOX

If we can narrow the legacy of George Müller to just one factor, it would have to be prayer. He is known as the man who relied entirely on faith, expressed in prayer, for the funding of his ministry. As he housed, fed, and raised thousands of England's neediest orphans, he steadfastly refused to raise funds—to beg, plead, or even ask for money. Instead, he prayed, and trusted God to provide. And God did provide in amazing ways. And because he did, Müller has inspired many others with the power of prayer.

Müller's legacy lives on today in the work of the George Müller Charitable Trust, and I made sure to set up an appointment so I could learn about their work. Before I arrived I visited nearby Ashley Down, where Müller's five great orphan houses still stand, though they have since been repurposed as flats and as facilities of the City of Bristol College. I marveled at the sheer size of them and tried to imagine what it must have been like when thousands of children lived in the dormitories, played on the grounds, and learned in the classrooms.

I was then welcomed into the offices of the trust, where they maintain a wonderful one-room museum that contains some of Müller's precious effects. I had the immense privilege of sitting at his desk to read some of the handwritten notes that fill pages of his well-worn Bible. I imagined him sitting there

Müller's collection box—
"For the orphans"

with the Bible open, penning a letter of love and encouragement to Hudson Taylor or preparing the sermon he would preach for Charles Spurgeon. I read letters in which he expressed his gratitude for financial gifts great and small (and in which he did not include a plea for them to give more).

But the object there that seemed to best tell the story of his life and legacy was a small wooden collection box. The lacquer has worn away in parts and become darkened in others. The dovetail joints that hold it together show through. The front says simply, "For the orphans." Müller would not ask people to give money but instead would pray for the Lord to provide. One of these boxes was placed within each of the orphan houses so that people could give as the Lord directed, each one perhaps inadvertently providing an answer to those earnest prayers. Those simple boxes aptly tell about the simple but expansive faith of a great man.

Sitting at George Müller's desk, reading his Bible

© Stephen McCaskell

28

BONNIE BRAE HOUSE
FRONT PORCH

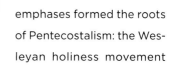

Pentecostalism is such an established fact of the Christian world today that we may be prone to forget that it is actually a recent development in the history of our faith. While various similar movements rose and fell away through the centuries, it was not until the early 1900s that the first true Pentecostals arose—the equivalent of appearing at the 95th meter of an Olympic 100-meter final or the forty-third minute of a forty-five-minute sermon. But the movement they began spread with great speed and soon spanned the globe. It went from a fringe to a mainstream expression of Christianity. I came across Pentecostals and Pentecostalism in nearly every country I visited, so I was eager to track down their origins. In the final weeks of my journey, I ventured to California to investigate the place where Pentecostalism began.

A number of personalities and theological emphases formed the roots of Pentecostalism: the Wesleyan holiness movement had led to a longing for complete sanctification; Charles Parham had begun to teach that the miraculous gifts described in the New Testament, especially the gift of tongues, should still be available to contemporary Christians; a number of Christians had developed a longing for a more personal experience of the Holy Spirit; a spirit of independence had led to churches eschewing denominational statements of faith in favor of their own.[1] In 1906 all of these threads came together in Richard and Ruth Asberry's little wooden house on Los Angeles's Bonnie Brae Street.

I visited 216 North Bonnie Brae Street early on a fine spring morning. The house is set on a little rise far above the street, surrounded by a tall fence and guarded by a gate. Although I had made and confirmed an appointment, that gate was shut and locked. I waited and waited, and my patience was at last rewarded when the house's caretaker arrived to lead me through. As I walked up the long flight of stairs, I spotted a sign on the front door that forbade photographs and instructed, "Please remove your footwear upon entering this holy place."

So what makes this place holy? It was here that the famed Azusa Street Revival began—the event that marks the beginning of modern Pentecostalism and the charismatic movement that grew out of it. In April 1906 Pastor William Seymour was leading his congregation through a ten-day fast in which they were praying for unusual evidence of the presence and power of the Holy Spirit. Suddenly several of them began to speak and sing in tongues. Out of necessity the services were moved to a different location, but the house has been preserved as both a museum and a kind of sanctuary where people come to pray for similar outpourings. The caretaker told me that just a few days prior she had witnessed some astounding miracles as God's healing power fell on the place.[2]

As she led me through the house, I found that there are few original artifacts—a piano still sits in the living room, along with a few other pieces of furniture. One room contains a pulpit that is labeled as belonging to Kathryn Kuhlman, though the caretaker said it had only

216 North Bonnie Brae Street, Los Angeles, CA,
the home of Richard and Ruth Asberry

just appeared in the house and she had no idea how it had gotten there. It is clear that the house's primary purpose is as a place of pilgrimage for those who hope to feel and experience the Holy Spirit in a powerful way. Many of them come to pray through the night, pleading for God to grant such favor.

But as I walked back out through the front door, something did catch my eye as I remembered an interesting part of the story of the Azusa Street Revival. On April 9, 1906, William Seymour and his little African American congregation were just three days into their ten-day fast when, during a private meeting, he laid hands on one of his congregants and prayed that he would receive the Holy Spirit. That man fell to the floor and began to speak in a language neither of them understood. This is what they had been hoping, longing, and praying for, so they hurried to this house where the rest of the congregation had gathered. Immediately several others had a similar experience of speaking or singing in tongues. In the days that followed, news spread through the neighborhood and people crowded into the home to witness these amazing events and to seek the gift for themselves. "This was no quiet demonstration; it was full of noisy manifestations, shouts, speaking in tongues, moaning, and singing in tongues."[3] Soon little Bonnie

I spent the whole year with a camera in my face.
© Aileen Challies

Brae House could contain no more people, so newcomers began to gather on the porch and look through the windows. Then, just a few days after the excitement began, the porch collapsed with a crash under their weight.[4] Looking down, I could see that it has clearly been rebuilt and is newer than the house.

That collapsed and rebuilt porch seemed especially significant, as if in its own way it tells the story of Pentecostalism. It tells how this sudden revival seemed to meet a longing for more, a longing for miraculous encounters with the Spirit of God, which is why so many people flocked to it. It tells how this revival spread at such breakneck speed that within days it had overflowed this house. Within days it would move to a new location, a vacant building on 312 Azusa Street. Within weeks it would spread across the city and the country, and within months across the world. Soon Christians across the globe were hearing about this revival and longing to experience it for themselves. Many who "caught the fire" took it with them. The Christian church was never the same.

The Azusa Street Revival did not continue for long. By 1909 it had begun to go into decline, and within a few years it had collapsed through scandal and infighting. But the movement continued and grew, so that today there are some five hundred million people in the world who identify as either Pentecostal or charismatic. Each of them, in some way, can trace their roots to this little home and this rebuilt porch in California.

I had one continent yet to visit. Although South America was largely colonized and subjugated by Roman Catholic powers, I knew it had since witnessed a remarkable growth in Protestantism. I was eager to track down one of the organizations responsible for this extraordinary story.

29
PAPALLACTA DAM

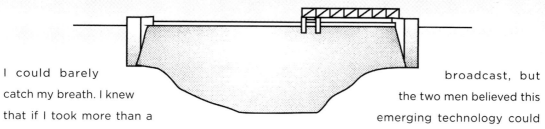

I could barely catch my breath. I knew that if I took more than a few, slow steps, I'd find myself gasping for air.

Standing on a hilltop at fourteen thousand feet of elevation, I was deep in the Ecuadorian Andes. It was clear that I hadn't taken enough time to acclimate to the elevation change. I gazed at the remarkable feat of engineering before me and marveled that anyone had been brave enough—or had the conviction and resources—to even attempt it, much less complete it. The engineering marvel before me was Lake Loreto dam, and it survives today as a testament to the great lengths God's people will go to get the gospel to those who have not yet heard it. It also tells us a story of the gospel's advance in Latin America.

On Christmas Day 1931, Clarence Jones and Reuben Larson sat before a small radio transmitter that had been erected in a home in Quito, Ecuador. They began to speak about Jesus, transmitting their words over the airwaves. At that time there were only six radio receivers in all of Ecuador even capable of receiving the broadcast, but the two men believed this emerging technology could be used to spread the good news of Jesus across the nation and the rest of the continent. They hoped that the technology would provide a means for millions of people to hear the gospel for the first time. They called their fledgling radio station HCJB—Heralding Christ Jesus' Blessings in English or Hoy Christo Jesús Bendice in Spanish.[1] The station grew over time, and soon they were able to purchase and install even more powerful transmitters. Their location in Quito—at a high elevation exactly on the equator—allowed them to broadcast not only to Central and South America but far beyond. Soon they were adding programming in other languages, shifting their focus to even more countries where the gospel message could be translated and shared.

But all of this growth led to some problems. The large transmitters demanded huge amounts of power, and the ministry couldn't afford to purchase the diesel fuel needed to run the generators. They brainstormed several ideas and landed on one: they could generate their own hydroelectric power. HCJB bought the rights to Lake Loreto, which rises high above the village of Papallacta some thirty miles from the ministry headquarters in Quito. After purchasing the lake, it fell to missionary Don Schroder to construct a dam. An early survey of the site showed that while it was a suitable location for a dam, it was inaccessible to vehicles.[2] Every worker, every piece of equipment, every stick of dynamite, and the endless tons of material needed to construct and maintain the dam would need to be carried over towering mountain peaks and across inhospitable terrain.

The missionaries hired local workers, purchased a host of pack mules, and set out to begin their work. They started in November 1969 and continued for more than a year, mostly in preparation. They first had to clear a trail to the site, and then create a camp and build cabins for the workers. Then they had to begin dredging tons of sand from the bottom of the lake and blasting a channel through solid rock, all of this at an elevation of fourteen thousand feet. When that work was completed, they could finally begin to mix the concrete and shape the dam. When the work at last came to an end, they had created a step-shaped dam that was 22 feet high and 150 feet across. Not a single worker had been seriously hurt during its construction, and at the very top of the structure they carefully inscribed these words:

Papallacta Dam
© *Stephen McCaskell*

"AGUA PARA LA GLORIA DIOS" ("water for the glory of God"). Far down the mountain they had already built a generating station and had installed a hydroelectric generator. They had strung cables that would carry the electricity to their transmitters more than thirty miles away. In a moving ceremony on March 22, 1971, they dedicated the work to the glory of God and the advance of his gospel. The dam was complete, the power was available, and the station could continue to transmit.

The Loreto Dam project was a resounding success. With the power it generated, HCJB was able to continue growing, and they installed even more powerful transmitters. Although the radio broadcasts could reach mainland Europe and much of Russia, the Middle East and parts of Asia, its greatest impact was still felt in South America, where HCJB broadcasted gospel programs twenty-four hours a day, seven days a week in Spanish, Portuguese, and a variety of local languages. The programming reached great cities and jungle villages alike with the message of salvation through Jesus Christ. For many people who had no access to Christian churches or other Christian believers, the radio became a lifeline, the means through which they came to Christ and were discipled for Christ. Only God knows how many of his people came to saving faith through that ministry.

The dam still stands today, though it has since been enlarged, and sadly, the inscription

High up in the Andes
© Stephen McCaskell

This was taken from the Papallacta Dam
and looks over Lake Loreto.

has been covered over. It continues to hold back the waters of Lake Loreto so they can be controlled to provide a steady source of power every day of the year. Although the generator installed many years ago continues to provide electricity, many of the radio transmitters have since been removed and the ministry has turned much of its programming focus to the internet. But as long as the dam remains, it will stand as a testament to the great effort and ingenuity of Christians as they carry out the Great Commission. In its own way, the dam gave me a glimpse of the way technology has been used to spread the gospel and a look at one way the good news has been shared specifically with the people of Latin America. It aptly shows how God so burdens people that they will go to extreme lengths to carry out his work and spread his message, sometimes face-to-face and sometimes through new technological marvels.

And after considering how the age-old gospel went south through exciting new technologies, I would next have to consider how a modern-day "gospel" sprang up in America and soon spread across the globe.

30

ORAL ROBERTS'S PRAYING HANDS

In a 2015 interview, Pastor Conrad Mbewe of Zambia lamented that a teaching known as the "prosperity gospel" had swept across Africa. "Everywhere, especially on radio and television, almost all you hear is this message about how God in Christ wants us to be physically healthy and materially prosperous. You hardly ever hear sermons about sin and repentance. So salvation has now become deliverance from sickness and poverty. It is temporal rather than eternal."[1] Around the same time, Dominican pastor Jairo Namnún was saying something similar: "While prosperity teachers are highly influential in the United States and other places, they're particularly popular in Latin America. In fact, the charismatic, Word-of-faith, prosperity form of Christianity is, by and large, the only form of Protestantism people know."[2] And sadly, as I traveled the world, I heard the same lament from pastors of persecuted churches in India and underground churches in China. John Piper, a popular American preacher and author, considers the prosperity gospel one of America's most prominent and shameful exports. "People are being destroyed by it. Christians are being weakened by it. God is being dishonored by it. And souls are perishing because of it."[3] Although this particular form of Christianity was unknown until the middle of the twentieth century, it has since spread at breakneck speed. I went looking for its origins in Tulsa, Oklahoma, at the university founded by the man who, more than any other, fabricated and spread it.

Oral Roberts was born in Oklahoma on January 24, 1918, the son of an early Pentecostal preacher. He was a rebellious child who fought his parents' fundamentalism, but a near-fatal case of tuberculosis, from which he claimed to be miraculously healed, led him to turn around and profess faith in Christ.[4] He soon committed his life to ministry and proved himself a capable speaker. For several years Roberts was a fixture at Pentecostal revivals, then the pastor of a fast-growing church. In 1947 he experienced a crisis of faith and was tempted to abandon Christianity altogether, but as he studied his Bible and prayed, he arrived at a pair of realizations that transformed him and charted a new course for his life.[5] He came to believe that God is not only interested in our spiritual well-being but also our financial prosperity. And just as important, he became convinced that the healing that God offers through the gospel is not only spiritual but also physical. Roberts went still further, claiming that God had revealed in a vision that he, Oral Roberts, had been given special divine power to heal others.[6]

Following this revelation, Roberts embarked on the career that would define him and have a deep impact on the wider church—his itinerant revival and healing ministry. Soon he was traveling across America and the world hosting great tent crusades. While he always insisted that his first concern was saving souls, countless millions attended his events to receive physical healing and financial prosperity. Most events began with a short time of singing, which was followed by a sermon and an altar call. As crowds surged forward and were ushered to a prayer tent, Roberts would slip away to visit the "invalid" section where the most seriously ill people awaited his touch.[7] As he did this, the people with more moderate afflictions would line up in the aisles. He would return to the main tent, take his place on a platform at the front of the crowd, and begin to touch and pray for as many people as possible, declaring them healed and whole. This was the blueprint his crusades would follow for many years and the pattern many imitators would follow.[8]

In the 1940s Roberts began to broadcast his sermons on the radio, but it was the 1950s and the rise of television that boosted his reputation and made him a household name. He quickly saw the possibilities of this new medium and bought massive amounts of airtime. The expenses forced him to get creative with fund-raising, and he created the concept of a "blessing pact" in which he would pray that those who gave to his ministry would receive exponentially more money over the next twelve months.[9] He also began to offer refunds for those who, after the twelve-month period, were not satisfied that God had prospered them. He would eventually go even further, continually innovating new ways to gather the funds to support his growing ambitions. These promises and other statements like them became mainstays of the movement he helped create. Soon many others who had observed his success followed, seeking to emulate his techniques and methods. Kenneth Copeland, Kenneth Hagin, Reinhard Bonnke, and John Osteen (father of Joel Osteen) were all at one time acolytes or friends of Roberts. As his fame grew, so did his wealth and, with it, his love for an extravagant and ostentatious lifestyle.

In 1963 he founded Oral Roberts University, and the school opened its doors two years later. I wanted to visit the school to see what it would tell me about this man and the message he proclaimed. Like any visitor to the campus, the first features I noticed were the giant praying hands at the entrance and the two-hundred-foot prayer tower at its center. The tower was of particular interest to me not only because of its iconic shape but also because I had heard it contains a few exhibits about Roberts's life and career. After taking the elevator to the top and viewing the campus from that vantage point, I went back down and browsed through the exhibits, which included a Bible and a collection of his sermon notes. On the wall were many letters from presidents and other notable historical figures, lauding Roberts or thanking him for his various contributions. Although I listened as closely as I could, there was nothing there that told me much of a story. I decided I'd return to the entrance and spend some time with those large praying hands. And if hands can speak, these did.

In the late 1970s Roberts declared that God had directed him to build a medical center he'd call the City of Faith. This center would be comprised of three buildings built adjacent to the ORU campus—one of them twenty stories tall, one of them thirty, and the third towering over them both at sixty. They would, for the first time, integrate the complementary powers of prayer and medicine. A project this ambitious would necessitate the raising of fantastic sums of money that would tax his limits. He would have to spar with local authorities who insisted they already had a surplus of available hospital beds. But he persisted, and the buildings were soon completed.

Roberts had commissioned a giant bronze sculpture of two hands together in the posture of prayer to sit before the entrance to the City of Faith. At the time, this was the largest cast-bronze sculpture in the world, and a brochure explained, "One hand represents the hand of prayer raised to God, the source of health and healing, and the other the hand of the physician raised in commitment to place all of God's healing power in operation for every patient

Bronze sculpture of praying hands
at Oral Roberts University

and against every disease."[10] The sculpture was an imposing and vivid representation of Roberts's theology but also of the vastness of his vision. They were meant to be a visual symbol of how the world would be transformed by this new integration of physical and spiritual healing, but they also displayed and symbolized Roberts's ability to believe God for something so vast as these three buildings. He went so far as to declare that even the cure for cancer would emerge from this new ministry.[11] The first patients were admitted in 1981.

By 1986 the hospital was hemorrhaging money and nearly vacant. Three years later the medical facilities were shuttered and the buildings leased out as office space. The City of Faith had failed catastrophically, dealing the ministry a serious blow to both its reputation and its finances. As for the prayer hands, they were hardly suited to the outside of an office tower, so they were removed to the nearby entrance to ORU. They remain there to this day. Visitors see them and marvel but often don't know the true story they tell. Sadly and ironically, the story is one of failure. It's a story of poor doctrine and manipulative tactics. It's a story of the short-term success but long-term failure of this prosperity gospel that makes such

My road took me through Arizona, where I snapped this fun shot.

great promises but wanders so far from the true gospel of Jesus Christ.

Although Roberts died in 2009 and his name has slowly begun to fade away, his doctrine remains more prominent than ever. His notions of seed faith and points of contact, his methods of sending people tokens and prayer hankies, his constant covenants and pacts to solicit support, are all the stuff of so many of today's televangelists. The hands clasped in prayer, memorialized in that great bronze statue, also reached into millions of pockets.

With these hands in my rearview mirror, I was ready to visit something far more encouraging, and to do that I'd need to head northwest to Idaho.

31
NATE SAINT'S AIRCRAFT

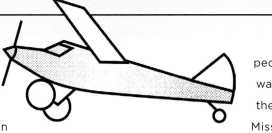

In just a few decades, the tale has become one of the best-known stories in the long history of Christian missions. On January 8, 1956, deep in the jungles of Ecuador, five young American missionaries were martyred as they attempted to bring the message of Jesus Christ to the native Huaorani people. Their deaths made headlines across the world. And as their story became known, it led a whole generation of Christians to acknowledge the world's desperate need for missionaries, inspiring countless thousands to take up the cause. In the mysterious providence of God, a few lives lost on one stony beach led to a great harvest of souls across a needy world. And today an amazing artifact in Idaho helps to pass on the story to a new generation.

Among the missionaries who died on the beach that day was Nate Saint, a pilot with Mission Aviation Fellowship (MAF). The seeds that would grow into MAF were planted during the Second World War as Christian pilots began to consider how their skills might be put to use in serving unreached and otherwise unreachable people groups. As the war drew to its close, the Christian Airmen's Missionary Fellowship (soon renamed Mission Aviation Fellowship) was founded in America. The following year Betty Greene flew its first plane on its first flight, transporting mission workers to a remote location in Mexico.[1]

Nate Saint joined MAF as a missionary pilot in 1948 and soon moved to Shell Mera, Ecuador, to help establish a new base of operations that would serve a host of unreached tribes.[2] Here he met Jim Elliot, Pete Fleming, Ed McCully, and Roger Youderian. Together they dreamed up Operation Auca, an effort to reach the Huaorani tribe—a people known for their fierceness and unwillingness to receive outsiders. To that point they were completely unreached by the gospel. Still, the missionaries believed this was God's calling on their lives. In the closing months of 1955, they scouted locations from the air, discovered Huaorani villages, and began to drop gifts from their aircraft. These gifts were eventually reciprocated, giving the men confidence that it

Rescue party at the site where the five missionaries were murdered by Auca (Waodani/Huarani) tribespeople on January 11, 1956 in the Amazon Basin jungle of Ecuador. The story was covered by LIFE magazine in January 1956.

Alpha Historica/Alamy Stock Photo

was time to make contact. On January 2 Saint shuttled the men to "Palm Beach" in his little Piper Family Cruiser aircraft. They waited there for three days before the first Huaorani appeared on the 6th, and for the next couple of days the meetings seemed to go well. But then on January 8, a party of warriors emerged from the jungle intent on defending themselves from what they perceived to be a deadly threat. Elliot was the first to be speared, with the others falling soon after. The Huaorani quickly faded into the jungle, abandoned their village, and disappeared.[3]

When the missionaries failed to report to their headquarters, another plane was sent to investigate, and the pilot spotted bodies in the river. Days later a team made up of both Ecuadorians and Americans made the arduous hike into the jungle to Palm Beach. Among them was *Life* photographer-correspondent Cornell Capa, who captured stunning images of the scene. These accompanied a lengthy feature in the January 30 issue of the magazine, which at that time was published weekly and ranked among the world's most popular and important periodicals.[4] Most of the content was excerpts of Saint's and Fleming's journals. They told of their love for Christ, their love for their fellow man, and their willingness to give all for that cause. They told of their excitement and their desire to see the Huaorani come to

Christ. Their journals ended ominously with reports of a forthcoming meeting, and it is here that Capa's photography told the tragic close to their story. He captured Youderian's body floating facedown in the river, a broken spear protruding from his hip. He captured the burial service, conducted hastily out of fear of another attack. Further photos showed the scene from the air, including Elliot's body downstream, caught up in a tangle of debris. The mission to the Huaorani had ended in disaster.

Or had it? The story of the mission to reach the Huaorani did not end that day, for Nate's sister, Rachel, and Jim's wife, Elisabeth, took up the work, establishing a new camp, reaching out to the Huaorani people, and eventually seeing many of them profess faith in Christ. This included several of those responsible for killing their loved ones. It is a powerful story, one that cannot be fully captured in this short recounting.[5]

But there is one aspect of the story, a further detail, that I do want to share with you

Nate Saint's aircraft

because it was so moving to me. In 1994, almost forty years after the death of the missionaries, a family was on Palm Beach when they spotted bits of Saint's aircraft protruding from the sand. Heavy rain had caused the river's course to shift, revealing portions of the lower fuselage. MAF missionaries, including Nate's son Steve came to the scene to excavate and, using metal detectors, found more remnants of the plane. They collected these and hauled them back to America.[6]

It was a cold winter's day when I arrived in Nampa, Idaho, where the headquarters of MAF can be found at the edge of the municipal airport. Walking through the doors, I immediately noticed the remnants of the plane in an exhibit behind the reception area. Although I was eager to see it, before I could take a closer look, a guide led me on a tour of the facilities. I was the lone visitor that day, so I got a private tour. We visited the hangers where a team of employees and volunteers continue to maintain MAF's fleet, modifying stock aircraft to suit the unique requirements of missionary aviation. I learned that MAF continues to operate around the world, including in a number of restricted-access countries where they've found ways to carry the gospel to areas out of bounds to other organizations. I learned that somewhere in the world an MAF aircraft takes off or lands every twelve minutes. Today MAF continues to serve the cause its founders created it for.

With my tour complete, I returned to the entrance to get a better look at Nate Saint's aircraft. Although it has the form of a complete fuselage, it's clear that many parts have been reconstructed, including new metal tubing that has been fused with the original to form the shape of a Piper Family Cruiser. A piece of the original cowling still bears the Piper branding, and nearby a few of the original controls remain in place. In at least one spot, the marks of a machete blade have gouged scars into the metal. On the ground is a bullhorn through which the missionaries spoke words of friendship and assurance as they attempted to gain the trust of the Huaorani.

Knowing the story of that day and the young lives lost, I found it to be a moving exhibit. Even though I'd had the chance to observe countless objects of Christian history, this one seems particularly significant. It tells the story of an important piece of recent Christian history. As I studied the plane, I was reminded of the men who flew on it, heading into unknown circumstances but trusting in their Lord. They were young men who risked their lives for the sake of the gospel of Jesus Christ, and who ultimately gave their lives to spark a whole new wave of missions. The apparent failure of their attempt was turned to success as it ignited a new wave of successful missionary endeavor. The zeal and faithfulness of these men challenged the apathy of a sleeping evangelical church, awakening many thousands more to follow Christ in mission. The aircraft is a fitting tribute to their love for their Savior and for those made in his image.

As he set out on Operation Auca, Nate

Saint wrote these words in his journal: "May God continue to put His good hand on the project and may we drop it when not fully assured of His direction. At present we feel unanimously that God is in it. May the praise be His and may it be that some Auca, clothed in the righteousness of Jesus Christ, will be with us as we lift our voice in praise before His throne."[7] In an unexpected way, his prayers were answered that day in January 1956.

Flying home from Idaho, I had a long lay-over in Chicago and decided to make the most of it by visiting the alma mater of the last great evangelist.

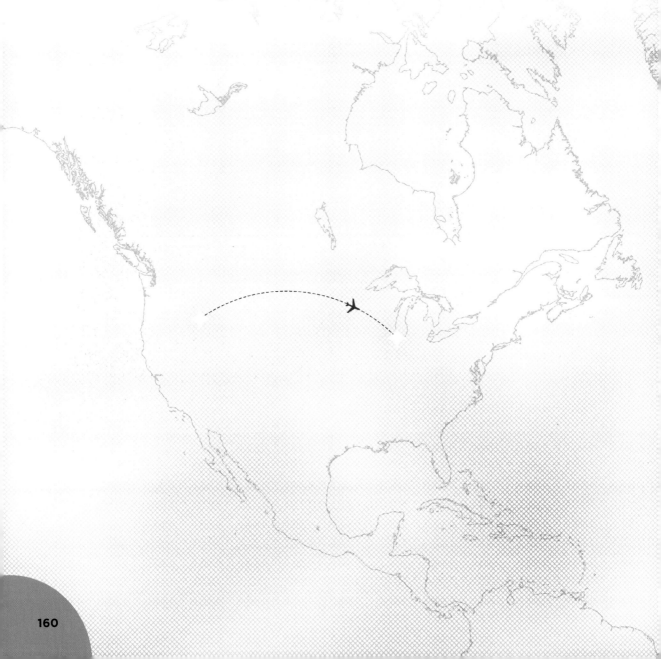

32

BILLY GRAHAM'S TRAVELING PULPIT

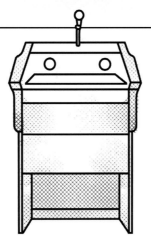

Telling the story of twentieth-century Christianity would be impossible without acknowledging the influence of Billy Graham. In a century rocked by two devastating global wars, many people across the Western world began to turn away from Christianity, no longer convinced it offered compelling answers to the questions of our modern times. Surveying the religious landscape, they saw cold traditionalism, bickering fundamentalism, and wandering liberalism. Many drifted away altogether from church commitment and religious conviction.

Few could have predicted the rise of a new kind of evangelist who would electrify great crowds with his simple gospel message, who would travel the world seeing countless numbers of people make professions of faith, and who would become known fondly as "America's Pastor." Few, least of all the man himself, could have foretold the rise, the prominence, and the ministry of Billy Graham. In fact, he

himself would later say, "I have often said that the first thing I am going to do when I get to heaven is to ask, 'Why me, Lord? Why did you choose a farm boy from North Carolina to preach to so many?'"[1]

Billy Graham was born in his family's farmhouse near Charlotte, North Carolina, on November 7, 1918. After professing faith in his teens, Graham decided to dedicate his life to preaching the gospel. He was educated at Florida Bible Institute and Wheaton College, then tried his hand at various ministries before concluding that his gifting was as an itinerant evangelist. Although he saw many people moved by his preaching, he remained relatively unknown until his 1949 crusade in Los Angeles. The newspaper magnate William Randolph Hearst commanded his reporters to "puff Billy Graham," and soon that crusade was overflowing with curious attenders, and organizers had to extend the event. (It was at this crusade that Louis Zamperini, later to be

Billy Graham Center Museum, Wheaton, IL
© Daniel X. O'Neil/Flickr, CC BY 2.0

the subject of a number of biographical books and the popular film *Unbroken*, came to faith.) Graham became a household name across America, and he would remain that way until his death (which, as it happens, came while I was on my long flight to Australia for this project—I landed to find my phone immediately lighting up with notifications and tributes).

Among all of Graham's crusades, none would define him as powerfully as the New York crusade of 1957. Graham's alma mater, Wheaton College, holds a key artifact from this crusade in their Billy Graham Center Museum. I visited the museum during a long layover in Chicago, making the lengthy and bumper-to-bumper drive from O'Hare International Airport to the suburb of Wheaton. Although the campus was buzzing with activity, I had the museum almost entirely to myself and enjoyed slowly browsing its many

exhibits. While the first half is dedicated to the history of Christianity in America, the entire second half focuses on Graham. Artifacts and exhibits tell of his lineage and childhood, his marriage and call to ministry. Then the floor opens up to a large area that begins to describe and display his many crusades. And in the center of it all is an object that was present for so much of his ministry, including the great crusade in New York—his traveling pulpit.

The New York crusade was originally meant to take place over six weeks, beginning on May 15, 1957. However, by the time it came to its end, it had lasted for sixteen weeks—nearly four months. Over that time, Graham preached at more than one hundred services and other events, and nearly 1.7 million people crammed into Madison Square Garden over the course of ninety-seven meetings, while other preaching events, including a packed-out crowd at Yankee Stadium, raised the total attendance past the two million mark. But the impact of that visit carried far beyond New York City. Beginning on June 1, television networks began to broadcast some of the services, and millions more tuned in that way.[2]

Portions of the crusade were filmed and are now widely available online. It is an interesting exercise to hear Graham preach his simple message and to consider how that message electrified great crowds. He is invariably warm and winsome in his demeanor, and there is just a little North Carolina in his accent and cadence. He tells the people about their spiritual insufficiency, warns them that they must prepare themselves for a coming judgment, tells them about Jesus, and calls them to make a decision for Jesus. In most cases he demands an outward sign of that commitment—coming forward for an altar call or simply raising a hand when space does not permit much movement. And in every case, it is obvious that great crowds have responded.

And as you watch this crusade, or any number of the ones that followed it, take a moment to look down just a little and you may notice that Graham usually preaches from the same wide wooden pulpit. This is the pulpit that is on display at Wheaton today, and visitors are welcome to examine it and even stand behind it. I did that very thing, pausing to really study it and to examine it from every side. Not surprisingly, it had its own story to tell.

This pulpit was a gift from Thomas J. Watson, the longtime chairman and CEO of IBM.[3]

Billy Graham's traveling pulpit

He had once observed Graham struggling to preach from a pulpit that was too small, so as an act of kindness he custom-crafted one he deemed more suitable. Graham was able to raise and lower it electrically and to increase or decrease the tilt of its lectern—significant innovations for the time. In this way different speakers and singers could use it comfortably at the same event. Five microphone sockets line its front edge, as if to show just how many people crowded to hear Graham's words. On the panel facing the preacher, I saw a clock and timer as well as three lights—one of which would illuminate to let Graham know he had five minutes left to preach, the next when he had two, and the third one when he was down to his final minute.[4] It's a hardy, customized traveling pulpit for a traveling evangelist, and for the prime years of his ministry, it went with Graham wherever he traveled and preached. Just imagine how many millions of people saw that pulpit—or perhaps, even better, how many didn't see that pulpit because their eyes were fixed on the man behind it. The pulpit was never meant to be noticed, never meant to be the star of the show. Rather, it was meant to serve a supporting role to one of history's foremost evangelists.

Graham's New York crusade generated massive crowds but also massive waves of critique. Liberal Protestants complained that Graham's evangelicalism was too concerned with conversions and not concerned enough with matters of social justice. Fundamentalists were concerned about Graham's growing ecumenism, for he continually broadened his circles, insisting that he would accept support and assistance from any group as long as they did not hinder his message. In this way he embraced and endorsed Roman Catholics, Pentecostals, and prosperity preachers alike.[5] Today the crusade symbolizes the rupture of evangelicals with both liberals and fundamentalists, and as Graham distanced himself from both camps, he helped coalesce a new evangelicalism—a moderate, centrist movement whose primary concern was the salvation of souls. "For Evangelicals, the Crusade was a major step in gaining self-confidence, empowerment, and acceptance as a significant national group, concerned not only to preach the Gospel of salvation through Christ, but to apply Christian belief to the life of the nation, even as Evangelicals often disagreed among themselves about what that meant."[6] As he stood in that pulpit and preached, Graham not only reached the hearts of individuals but changed the very landscape of Christianity.

The crusade had taxed Graham, and many years later he would say that he never fully recovered from it. Yet during that time he emerged as the leader and de facto spokesman for American evangelicals. Americans were drawn to his kindness and sincerity, and he left New York as America's best-known and best-loved Christian leader. He was the first modern "crusader" who could gather great crowds of unbelievers, preach the gospel to them, and see thousands make a commitment for Christ. He made an indelible impact in America and globally, and that custom-built pulpit is an apt symbol of his ministry, a ministry dominated by preaching. With the emergence of Graham, evangelicalism was now a dominant force in American Christianity, and its effect was being felt all over the world.

Billy Graham's pulpit was the final *physical* object I would see on my journey. But I knew there was still at least one object left, an object that would aptly represent the twenty-first-century church. If Billy Graham can stand in as the last of the crusaders, the last of a generation of preachers, this next object can stand in as a token of the present and future.

33

YOUVERSION BIBLE APP

Craig Groeschel founded Life. Church in Oklahoma City, Oklahoma, in 1996. He and a handful of congregants began to meet in a small double-car garage lit with nothing more than a pair of twenty-dollar construction lights. Very quickly, though, the little church experienced explosive growth and was forced to move to a larger location. Today Life.Church is a multisite church that reaches tens of thousands of people every weekend through their many physical locations and their online presence. Collectively, they are considered the second-largest church in America.

In 2006 Groeschel and his team developed the idea to create an online Bible that might uniquely reach this new digital world. At that time Twitter was in its infancy, Facebook had just begun opening registrations to the broader public, having previously been reserved solely for college students, and YouTube was slowly becoming a household name. The people at Life.Church realized that the world was rapidly changing through these technological shifts, and the church would be forced to adapt. They found themselves thinking back to the days of the printing press when, for the first time in history, the Bible suddenly became widely available to the public. They understood that another communications revolution was underway and began to consider how they could take advantage of this digital explosion to distribute the world's most popular and important book.[1]

They had big dreams. They dreamed of more than merely distributing the Bible in digital form. They wanted a way to allow readers to have access to the Bible in every possible language, to interact with it, annotate it, and share it, and to form a global community of Bible readers and Bible lovers. Although we've

This is a photo I took of Lake Ontario just a few minutes from my home.

come to expect that level of access and interactivity today, this was groundbreaking in 2006. They called their dream YouVersion.[2]

The team at Life.Church developed YouVersion.com and, having secured relationships with various Bible publishers, launched the site in September 2007. They waited in hopeful anticipation and were surprised—and a little disappointed—to see that the response was muted. There was little interest in a digital Bible website. Although Groeschel and his team were tempted to give up, they felt that they should attempt one more avenue for their project—the creation of a mobile version of the site. They had begun observing that people were migrating from desktop computers to mobile devices like iPods and smartphones, and a new device called the "iPhone" had just been unveiled. They wondered what possibilities might come with this newfound mobility, and Apple's new iTunes app store provided the perfect means for distribution, so Life.Church rapidly developed their Bible App and gave it away free of charge.[3] They anticipated perhaps a hundred thousand downloads in the first year. There were eighty thousand in the first three days alone.

Even better, they found that people were not only downloading and installing the app but actually using it. People were reading the Bible, looking up passages, and sharing what they learned with their friends. Very quickly the developers began to add new languages, new translations, and new features. And the rest, as they say, is history.

As I write these words, the YouVersion Bible App has been installed on almost four hundred million devices, and it is just one of a host of Bible apps. Its users read over twenty-seven billion chapters of the Bible every year and listen to another four billion chapters. The app offers 1,841 Bible versions that together represent 1,276 languages. It has become the kind of resource Christians in other times could not possibly have imagined.[4]

And unlike every other object in this book and on my journey around the world, the YouVersion Bible App gave me nowhere to visit, nothing to see. Anytime I want, I can pull my phone out of my pocket and gain full access to the app. And that's just the point, isn't it? The YouVersion App represents a new era in the history of the church. The digital revolution is an entirely new phenomenon, the creation of resources and materials that are unlike the physical objects that have come before. And this shift is changing everything. Most importantly, it is changing the way people read and experience God's Word.

Our brief (and very limited) survey of church history has shown that for most of the history of Christianity, access to God's Word has been scarce. Historically the Bible has been both rare and expensive. But in a digital world, the Bible can be infinitely duplicated and distributed at no cost. We live in a time of transition, from an era of Bible scarcity to an era of Bible abundance. As the internet extends to the farthest reaches of the earth, so, too, does the reach of God's Word. YouVersion is just one of countless thousands of apps that is taking the Word to the people.

Although it is time for this book, and our journey together, to draw to a close, it is interesting to consider where we began and where we are today. We end in a world so very different from the world that birthed the Christian church. But our time, too, is filled with promise and possibility. God has promised that his Word has always been living and active, sharper than any two-edged sword. If God has worked so powerfully when his Word has been rare and expensive, I can only imagine how he will work in this time, when the Bible can so easily be read and shared with billions of people. I can only begin to imagine how God will glorify himself in a world like this.

ACKNOWLEDGMENTS

The people to whom I owe the greatest gratitude, and the ones to whom I dedicate this book, are my wife and children. Although they were excited about this project and incredibly supportive of it, they made the sacrifice of letting me be gone for journey after journey. So Aileen, Nick, Abby, and Michaela, thank you. Now let's go enjoy all those travel miles I earned along the way.

I need to thank Stephen McCaskell for accompanying me on this journey. Stephen and I began the project as strangers (we met for the first time on the way to our first destination!) but ended as friends. Stephen, you proved the ultimate travel companion, and together we had an unforgettable year. Let's do it again sometime!

I also need to thank the generous people who made this journey possible. I won't name names because I know the only recognition you want is the "Well done, good and faithful servant" that you will hear someday. And I know you will.

I am also thankful to the team at Zondervan for supporting the project. Ryan and Jesse, working with you on yet another project has been a pleasure. You made this a better book.

And then there are so many people—too many to name—who helped me along the way. Some opened your homes to me, some helped me track down objects and experts, some spent two or three days driving me from place to place, some set up events that allowed me to meet local believers and enjoy Christian fellowship. Although I spent so much time away from home, I rarely felt like a stranger. I am so thankful to each one of you.

End of the journey

NOTES

Introduction

1. In fact, some years prior I had written a blog series on them—I attempted to trace the history of Christianity through objects—yet without actually visiting any of them. Some of these chapters are actually based on the work I did back then, though in every case, I visited the objects to do original research.
2. Except Antarctica. Even then I tried but could not find any objects noteworthy enough to make a tremendously distant, difficult, and costly journey.

Chapter 1: Augustus of Prima Porta

1. Nick Needham, *2000 Years of Christ's Power, Volume 1* (Ross-shire, UK: Christian Focus, 2016), 43.
2. Adrian Goldsworthy, *Pax Romana* (London: Weidenfeld & Nicolson, 2016), 13.
3. Josho Brouwers, *"Augustus of Prima Porta,"* Ancient World Magazine, January 8, 2018, www.ancientworldmagazine.com/articles/augustus-prima-porta/.
4. "The Statue of *Augustus of Prima Porta*," *Augustus of Prima Porta*, updated October 2005, http://web.mit.edu/21h.402/www/primaporta/description/breastplate/.
5. Brouwers, *"Augustus of Prima Porta."*

Chapter 2: John Rylands Manuscript P52

1. "St. John Fragment: How Was the Fragment Discovered?" The University of Manchester Library, www.library.manchester.ac.uk/search-resources/special-collections/guide

-to-special-collections/st-john-fragment/how-was-the-fragment-discovered/.
2. "P⁵²: A Fragment of the Gospel of John," K. C. Hanson.com, www.kchanson.com/ANCDOCS/greek/johnpap.html.
3. Formatting is drawn from "Rylands Library Papyrus P52," Wikipedia, https://en.wikipedia.org/wiki/Rylands_Library_Papyrus_P52.
4. "St. John Fragment: What Is the Significance of This Fragment?" The University of Manchester Library, www.library.manchester.ac.uk/search-resources/special-collections/guide-to-special-collections/st-john-fragment/what-is-the-significance/.
5. Bruce Metzger, *The Text of the New Testament* (New York: Oxford University Press, 1992), 39.

A Quick Look: The Pilate Stone

1. "Latin Dedicatory Inscription Mentioning Pontius Pilate, the Procurator of Judea," Israel Museum, Jerusalem, www.imj.org.il/en/collections/395572.

Chapter 3: Alexamenos Graffito

1. I probably should have looked at more of the TripAdvisor reviews, because many of them mentioned seemingly random, unexplained closures.
2. "The Alexamenos Graffito," NT Resources, http://ntresources.com/blog/?page_id=2669.

Chapter 4: Dogmatic Sarcophagus

1. Bizarrely, this object was also unexpectedly and randomly off-limits both times I visited, though I did at least manage to persuade curators to let me see it.

2. "'Dogmatic' Sarcophagus," Musei Vaticani, www.museivaticani.va/content/museivaticani/en/collezioni/musei/museo-pio-cristiano/sarcofagi-_a-doppio-registro/sarcofago-_dogmatico.html.

3. "The Dogmatic Sarcophagus," Christian Iconography, www.christianiconography.info/sicily/sarcDogmatic.html.

4. This is not the time or place to discuss the appropriateness of portraying God, and we will focus on the sarcophagus just as a key historical object.

5. "Constantine: First Christian Emperor," Christianity Today, www.christianitytoday.com/history/people/rulers/constantine.html.

6. Tim Dowley, *Introduction to the History of Christianity*, 3rd ed. (Minneapolis: Fortress, 2018), 112.

7. Nick Needham, *2000 Years of Christ's Power, Volume 1* (Ross-shire, UK: Christian Focus, 2016), 219.

8. Tim Dowley, *Introduction to the History of Christianity*, 2nd ed. (Minneapolis: Fortress, 2013), 119.

Chapter 5: Book of Kells

1. Nick Needham, *2000 Years of Christ's Power, Volume 1* (Ross-shire, UK: Christian Focus, 2016), 339.

2. Peter Yeoman and Nicki Scott, *Iona: Official Souvenir Guide* (Edinburgh: Historic Scotland, 2011), 59.

3. "The Book of Kells," The Library of Trinity College Dublin, www.tcd.ie/library/manuscripts/book-of-kells.php.

4. It can currently be viewed in its entirety here: https://digitalcollections.tcd.ie/home/index.php?DRIS_ID=MS58_003v.

5. "The Book of Kells TCD MS. 58," Celtic Studies Resources, www.digitalmedievalist.com/things/manuscripts/book-of-kells/.

6. Needham, *2000 Years of Christ's Power, Volume 1*, 265.

7. By comparison, today's editions are often revised every few years, and language that is even twenty years old is often considered archaic.

Chapter 6: Jan Hus's Cell Door

1. Bruce Shelley, *Church History in Plain Language* (Nashville: Thomas Nelson, 2013), 240.

2. Nick Needham, *2000 Years of Christ's Power, Volume 2* (Ross-shire, UK: Christian Focus, 2016), 420.

3. Needham, *2000 Years of Christ's Power, Volume 2*, 422.

4. Diana Kleyn with Joel R. Beeke, *Reformation Heroes* (Grand Rapids: Reformation Heritage, 2009), 21.

5. Shelley, *Church History in Plain Language*, 242.

6. Needham, *2000 Years of Christ's Power, Volume 2*, 423.

7. Needham, *2000 Years of Christ's Power, Volume 2*, 426.

Chapter 7: Gutenberg Bible

1. Hellmut E. Lehmann-Haupt, "Johannes Gutenberg," Encyclopaedia Britannica, www.britannica.com/biography/Johannes-Gutenberg.

2. "History of the Gutenberg Bible," Gutenberg Bible.com, www.gutenberg-bible.com/history.html.

3. I also saw Gutenberg Bibles at Yale University's Beinecke Library and at the British Library.

4. Tim Dowley, *Introduction to the History of Christianity*, 2nd ed. (Minneapolis: Fortress, 2013), 300.

Chapter 8: Erasmus's New Testament

1. Nick Needham, *2000 Years of Christ's Power, Volume 3* (Ross-shire, UK: Christian Focus, 2016), 37.

2. Needham, *2000 Years of Christ's Power, Volume 3*, 37–38.

3. Joseph C. Sommer, "Definition of Humanism," American Humanist Association, https://americanhumanist.org/what-is-humanism/definition-of-humanism/.

4. Robert Grudin, "Humanism," Encyclopaedia Britannica, www.britannica.com/topic/humanism.

5. Tim Dowley, *Introduction to the History of Christianity*, 2nd ed. (Minneapolis: Fortress, 2013), 395.

6. Preserved Smith, *Erasmus: A Study of His Life, Ideals and Place in History* (New York: Fred Ungar, 1962), 183–84.

7. Don't leave the room without pausing to look at the other books and at the armor the Swiss Reformer Zwingli was wearing when he was killed.

Chapter 9: Indulgence Box

1. The International Museum of the Reformation in Geneva, Switzerland, is the other contender for the crown. Do visit either one if you have the opportunity.

2. Luther's story has been told repeatedly over the past five hundred years. Perhaps the best current biography is Herman Selderhuis, *Martin Luther* (Wheaton: Crossway, 2017).

3. "Martin Luther," Christian Classics Ethereal Library, www.ccel.org/ccel/luther.

4. This is something to keep in mind if you visit Rome. St. Peter's is considered a must-see in Rome, but don't forget the context in which the money was raised to rebuild and beautify it.

5. Obviously those doors would have made a wonderful object for this project, but the ones you can see now are reproductions, not the originals.

6. "Martin Luther," Greatsite.com, Greatsite.com/timeline-english-bible-history/martin-luther.html.

Chapter 10: Tyndale New Testament

1. Gail Fineberg, "Let There Be Light: Exhibition Spotlights William Tyndale, English Martyr," Library of Congress, www.loc.gov/loc/lcib/9707/tyndale.html.

2. "William Tyndale's New Testament," British Library, www.bl.uk/collection-items/william-tyndales-new-testament.

3. "William Tyndale's New Testament."

4. The Treasures Gallery also holds the only remaining portion of this first attempt.

5. "William Tyndale's New Testament."

6. Peter Ackroyd, *Tudors* (New York: St. Martin's, 2013), 47.

7. Brian Moynahan, *God's Bestseller* (New York: St. Martin's, 2002), 1.

8. John Piper, "The Underground Translator," Desiring God, desiringgod.org/articles/the-underground-translator.

Chapter 11: Calvin's Chair

1. I've seen this widely attributed to Mark Noll but have not been able to verify it or locate the source.

2. Nick Needham, *2000 Years of Christ's Power, Volume 3* (Ross-shire, UK: Christian Focus, 2016), 202–4.

3. G. R. Evans, *The Roots of the Reformation* (Downers Grove, IL: IVP Academic, 2012), 341.

4. Steven Lawson, *The Expository Genius of John Calvin* (Lake Mary, FL: Reformation Trust, 2007), 21.

5. The *Institutes* is daunting, so perhaps begin with the wonderful excerpt *A Little Book on the Christian Life*. I recommend the edition translated by Burk Parsons and Aaron Denlinger (Sanford, FL: Reformation Trust, 2017).

6. Just within the gates of the cemetery you'll find a map that will help you locate Calvin's monument.

Chapter 12: The Triumph of Faith over Heresy

1. Various, *The Jesuits in Rome* (Rome: Iniziative Speciali di De Agostini Libri, 2014), 21.

2. Various, *Jesuits in Rome*, 21.

3. Nick Needham, *2000 Years of Christ's Power, Volume 3* (Ross-shire, UK: Christian Focus, 2016), 455.

4. In Poland, for example, the Reformation quickly gained many followers but was suppressed almost out of existence under the leadership of the Jesuits.

Chapter 13: Thomas Cranmer's Shackle

1. And, of course, several others. Nick Needham, *2000 Years of Christ's Power, Volume 3* (Ross-shire, UK: Christian Focus, 2016), 383.

2. Needham, *2000 Years of Christ's Power, Volume 3*, 391.

3. Peter Ackroyd, *Tudors* (New York: St. Martin's, 2012), 208.

4. John Foxe probably deserves his own chapter in this book for his *Acts and Monuments* (or *Foxe's Book of Martyrs*). A beautiful example is on display at the Museum of the Bible in Washington, DC.

5. John Foxe, *The Acts and Monuments of John Foxe, Volume VIII* (London: R. B. Seeley & W. Burnside, 1839), 90.

Chapter 14: St. Giles' Pulpit

1. Nick Needham, *2000 Years of Christ's Power, Volume 3* (Ross-shire, UK: Christian Focus, 2016), 401–2.

2. Jane Dawson, *John Knox* (New Haven, CT: Yale University Press, 2016), 32.

3. Douglas Bond, *The Mighty Weakness of John Knox* (Lake Mary, FL: Reformation Trust, 2011), 18.

4. Dawson, *John Knox*, 38.

5. There is some dispute about whether this was the pulpit Knox preached from, or if this one fell between the one he used and the one that is there today. Historians continue to research the issue. What is beyond dispute is that this is a very old pulpit that stood in St. Giles' at or near Knox's time.

Chapter 15: King James Bible

1. Peter Ackroyd, *Rebellion* (New York: St. Martin's, 2014), 35.

2. Nick Needham, *2000 Years of Christ's Power, Volume 4* (Ross-shire, UK: Christian Focus, 2016), 216–17.

3. "First Australian Penal Colony Established," History, November 13, 2009, www.history.com/this-day-in-history/first-australian-penal-colony-established.

4. "Australia," Encyclopaedia Britannica, www.britannica.com/place/Australia/History.

5. "Johnson, Richard (1753–1827)," Australian Dictionary of Biography, http://adb.anu.edu.au/biography/johnson-richard-2275.

A Quick Look: Defiled Tongan Idols

1. "Goddess Figure," Auckland Museum, www.aucklandmuseum.com/collections-research/collections/record/am_humanhistory-object-58762?k=goddess%20tonga&ordinal=2.

2. "Goddess Figure."

Chapter 16: William Brewster's Chest

1. "William Brewster," Encyclopaedia Britannica, www.britannica.com/biography/William-Brewster.

2. Nathaniel Philbrick, *Mayflower* (New York: Penguin, 2006), 162.

3. Francis J. Bremer, "Brewster, William," American National Biography, www.anb.org/abstract/10.1093/anb/9780198606697.001.0001/anb-9780198606697-e-0100102?rskey=m3pHNd&result=2.

Chapter 17: John Bunyan's Jug

1. As I edited this chapter in the church office, the associate pastor pulled a bag off the shelf and asked, "What's in this?" He then pulled out twelve copies of *The Pilgrim's Progress*.

2. "Puritanism," Encyclopaedia Britannica, www.britannica.com/topic/Puritanism.

3. John Bunyan, *Grace Abounding to the Chief of Sinners* (London: The Religious Tract Society, 1905), 229.

4. Bunyan, *Grace Abounding*, 327.

5. Faith Cook, *Fearless Pilgrim* (Darlington, UK: Evangelical, 2008), 192.

Chapter 18: Marie Durand's Inscription

1. The great majority of information about Marie Durand is in French. To my knowledge, the only English language biography is Simonetta Carr's work for children. Sadly, a full-length work was interrupted by the death of its author. The great majority of the information in this chapter is drawn from Carr.

2. Simonetta Carr, *Marie Durand* (Grand Rapids: Reformation Heritage, 2015), 12.

3. Carr, *Marie Durand*, 20.

4. Placards throughout the tower and along the nearby city walls tell the history of the tower and its occupants.

5. Carr, *Marie Durand*, 46.

Chapter 19: Whitefield Rock

1. John Tyson, *Assist Me to Proclaim* (Grand Rapids: Eerdmans, 2007), 230.

2. Bruce Shelley, *Church History in Plain Language* (Nashville: Thomas Nelson, 2013), 351.

3. David Fitzgerald, "Religion in Early West Brookfield," West Brookfield Historical Commission, http://westbrookfield.org/wp-content/uploads/2016/03/Religion-in-Early-West-Brookfield.pdf.

4. Michael A. G. Haykin, *The Revived Puritan* (Guelph, ON: Joshua, 2000), 32.

A Quick Look: Jonathan Edwards's Lazy Susan Desk

1. Jonathan Gibson, "Jonathan Edwards: A Missionary?," *Themelios* 36.3 (November 2011), http://themelios.thegospelcoalition.org/article/jonathan-edwards-a-missionary.

2. "Lazy Susan Table," Omohundro Institute of Early American History, *William and Mary Quarterly*, 3d. ser. 69, no. 4 (October 2012), https://oieahc-cf.wm.edu/wmq/Oct12/edwards/PDF/LazySusan_Supplement.pdf.

3. Matthew Everhard, "Freedom of the Will: Understanding Jonathan Edwards's Most Difficult Treatise," Edwards Studies, November 30, 2016, https://edwardsstudies.com/2016/11/.

Chapter 20: Charles Wesley's Organ

1. Faith Cook, *Selina, Countess of Huntingdon* (Edinburgh: Banner of Truth Trust, 2001), 18.

2. John Tyson, *Assist Me to Proclaim* (Grand Rapids: Eerdmans, 2007), 46.

Chapter 21: Selina Hastings's Memorial Token

1. Gilbert W. Kirby, *The Elect Lady* (Rushden: The Trustees of the Countess of Huntingdon's Connexion, 1972), 14.

2. Faith Cook, *Selina, Countess of Huntingdon* (Edinburgh: Banner of Truth Trust, 2001), 36.

3. Cook, *Selina*, 406.

4. Cook, *Selina*, 420.

Chapter 22: Brookes Slave Ship Model

1. William Hague, *William Wilberforce* (London: HarperCollins, 2007), 8–19.

2. Hague, *Wilberforce*, 42.

3. Hague, *Wilberforce*, 78.

4. Hague, *Wilberforce*, 88. There are many times in church history in which I would love to have been a fly on the wall, and this meeting is near the top of the list!

5. Hague, *Wilberforce*, 93.

6. "The 'Brookes' Slave Ship Model," The British Museum, BBC, www.bbc.co.uk/ahistoryoftheworld/objects/TrVw1QSnSKyRI59LC2csxg.

7. They were printed in such vast numbers that they are not particularly difficult to track down. The other great symbol of abolition was the Wedgwood antislavery medallion, one of which I noticed in a display case at the British Museum.

A Quick Look: Lemuel Haynes's Sermon Manuscript

1. Mark Sidwell, "The First Heroes of African American Christian History," *Christian History* 62 (1999), www.christianitytoday.com/history/issues/issue-62/black-christianity-before-civil-war-gallery-fruit-of.html.

Chapter 23: Andrew Fuller's Snuffbox

1. Bruce Shelley, *Church History in Plain Language* (Nashville: Thomas Nelson, 2013), 391.

2. John Piper, "His Suffering Sparked a Movement: David Brainerd (1718–1747)," Desiring God, April 20, 2018, www.desiringgod.org/articles/his-suffering-sparked-a-movement.

3. "William Carey (Missionary)," Wikipedia, https://en.wikipedia.org/wiki/William_Carey_(missionary).

4. Mark Galli, *131 Christians Everyone Should Know* (Nashville: Broadman & Holman, 2000), 246.

Chapter 24: The Slave Bible

1. All of the information in this article was drawn from the placards, videos, and other information within the exhibit. Museum employees were unable to direct me to other relevant sources of information.

2. A digital edition is available here: https://archive.org/details/selectpartsholy00unkngoog/page/n5.

A Quick Look: Josiah Henson

1. Jared A. Brock, *The Road to Dawn* (New York: PublicAffairs, 2018).
2. Tim Challies, "The Road to Dawn," *Challies*, May 23, 2018, challies.com/book-reviews/the-road-to-dawn/.
3. Brock, *Road to Dawn*, 14–16.
4. Brock, *Road to Dawn*, 80.
5. "Uncle Tom's Cabin Historic Site," Ontario Heritage Trust, www.heritagetrust.on.ca/en/properties/uncle-toms-cabin/history.
6. As detailed in W. B. Hartgrove, "The Story of Josiah Henson," *The Journal of Negro History* 3.1 (January 1918): 1–21, JSTOR, www.jstor.org/stable/2713789?seq=11#metadata_info_tab_contents.
7. Brock, *Road to Dawn*, 234.
8. Hartgrove, "Story of Josiah Henson," 11.

Chapter 25: David Livingstone's Writing Box

1. Stephen Tomkins, *David Livingstone* (Oxford: Lion Hudson, 2013), 11.
2. Rob Mackenzie, *David Livingstone: The Truth behind the Legend* (Ross-shire, UK: Christian Focus, 1993), 29.
3. Mackenzie, *Livingstone*, 47.
4. Do take the time to search for Livingstone's journals online and read some excerpts. It's not hard to see why his writing became so popular.
5. George Albert Shepperson, "David Livingstone: Scottish Explorer and Missionary," Encyclopaedia Britannica, www.britannica.com/biography/David-Livingstone.

Chapter 26: Amy Carmichael's Plaques

1. Iain Murray, *Amy Carmichael* (Edinburgh: Banner of Truth, 2015), 4–5.
2. Murray, *Carmichael*, 19.
3. Frank L. Houghton, "The Last Defile," in *Amy Carmichael of Dohnavur* (Fort Washington, PA: CLC, 2013), n.p.
4. Houghton, "The Last Defile."

Chapter 27: Hudson Taylor's Grave

1. Vance Christie, *Hudson Taylor* (Phillipsburg, NJ: P&R, 2011), 19.
2. Dr. and Mrs. Hudson Taylor, *Hudson Taylor's Spiritual Secret* (Chicago: Moody, 2009), 23.
3. "James Hudson Taylor, an English Missionary Who Made His Mark in China," Post Magazine, www.scmp.com/magazines/post-magazine/article/1835048/james-hudson-taylor-english-missionary-who-made-his-mark.
4. "Hudson and Maria Taylor's Graves Found in China," OMF, June 1, 2013, https://omf.org/nz/2013/06/01/hudson-and-maria-taylors-graves-found-in-china/.

Chapter 28: Bonnie Brae House Front Porch

1. Gaston Espinosa, *William J. Seymour and the Origins of Global Pentecostalism* (Durham, NC: Duke University Press, 2014), 42.
2. Espinosa, *Seymour*, 55.
3. Cecil M. Robeck Jr., *The Azusa Street Mission and Revival* (Nashville: Thomas Nelson, 2006), 69.
4. Robeck, *Azusa*, 69.

Chapter 29: Papallacta Dam

1. Lois Neely, *Come Up to This Mountain* (Colorado Springs: HCJB World Radio, 1998), 88.
2. Don Schroder, *Give Me This Mountain* (Orange, CA: Promise, 1996), 10. This book narrates the whole story of the building of the Loreto Dam and is my source for what follows.

Chapter 30: Oral Roberts's Praying Hands

1. Conrad Mbewe, "Prosperity Teaching Has Replaced True Gospel in Africa," The Gospel Coalition, June 25, 2015, www.thegospelcoalition.org/article/prosperity-teaching-has-replaced-true-gospel-in-africa/.
2. Jairo Namnún, "Encountering Prosperity Theology in Latin America," The Gospel Coalition, June 19, 2015, www.thegospelcoalition.org/article/the-prosperity-gospel-in-latin-america/.
3. John Piper, "Why I Abominate the Prosperity Gospel," Desiring God, October 29, 2008, www.desiringgod.org/interviews/why-i-abominate-the-prosperity-gospel.
4. David Edwin Harrell Jr., *Oral Roberts* (Bloomington: Indiana University Press, 1985), 34.

5. Harrell, *Roberts*, 66.

6. Harrell, *Roberts*, 67.

7. See an example at www.youtube.com/watch?v=MGBr2mtFw2E.

8. Harrell, *Roberts*, 95.

9. Jim Ernest Hunter Jr., "Where My Voice Is Heard Small," *Spiritus: ORU Journal of Theology* 3.1 (2018): 241.

10. Harrell, *Roberts*, 382.

11. Wayne Biddle and Margo Slade, "Oral Roberts's Word on Cancer, *New York Times*, January 30, 1983, www.nytimes.com/1983/01/30/weekin review/ideas-and-trends-oral-roberts-s-word -on-cancer.html.

Chapter 31: Nate Saint's Aircraft

1. "MAF History," Mission Aviation Fellowship, www.maf.org/about/history.

2. "Nate Saint," Mission Aviation Fellowship, www.maf.org/about/history/nate-saint.

3. Steve Saint, "Did They Have to Die?," *Christianity Today*, September 16, 1996, www.christianity today.com/ct/1996/september16/missionaries -did-they-have-to-die.html.

4. *Life*, January 30, 1956. MAF publishes and distributes an edition of this issue that contains only the cover and the ten pages covering the deaths of the missionaries.

5. More recently, Christians have realized that the narrative was set largely by Elisabeth Elliot and her book *Through Gates of Splendor*. Historians have been revisiting the events to try to tell them from a more objective perspective, including the perspective of the Huaorani. Still, the fact remains that between 1956 and today the story has been understood in this way.

6. Kenneth D. Macharg, "Martyrs' Lost Plane Recovered in Ecuador," *Christianity Today*, August 15, 1994, www.christianitytoday.com/ct/ 1994/august15/4t9057.html.

7. Excerpted from MAF's edition of *Life*'s January 30, 1956, issue.

Chapter 32: Billy Graham's Traveling Pulpit

1. Janet Chismar, "Lessons on Turning 92," Billy Graham Evangelistic Association, November 5, 2010, https://billygraham.org/story/ lessons-on-turning-92/.

2. "Authorized News Release from the Billy Graham New York Crusade, Inc.," Wheaton College, 2005, www2.wheaton.edu/bgc/archives/ exhibits/NYC57/20sample110-1.htm.

3. Marshall Frady, *Billy Graham: A Parable of American Righteousness* (New York: Simon & Schuster, 2006), 507.

4. Mary Bishop, *Billy Graham, the Man and His Ministry* (New York: Grosset & Dunlap, 1978), 36.

5. "Madison Sq. Garden NY Crusade 1957," Wheaton College, 2005, www2.wheaton.edu/ bgc/archives/exhibits/NYC57/20readmore.htm.

6. "Madison Sq. Garden."

Chapter 33: YouVersion Bible App

1. "Celebrating 10 Years of the YouVersion Bible App," Life.Church, 2019, www.life .church/media/stories/celebrating-10-years -of-the-youversion-bible-app/.

2. Robert Crosby, "The Bible Appreneur: An Interview with Bobby Gruenewald, Founder of YouVersion," June 19, 2012, www.patheos.com/ Evangelical/Bible-Appreneur-Robert-Crosby-06 -20-2012.html.

3. "Celebrating 10 Years of the YouVersion Bible App."

4. "2018 Year in Review," YouVersion, https://share .bible.com/2018/.

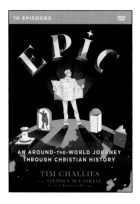